Rick and Bubba's Guide
to the
Almost Nearly Perfect Marriage

by

Rick Burgess and Bill "Bubba" Bussey

with Martha Bolton

THOMAS NELSON
Since 1798

NASHVILLE   DALLAS   MEXICO CITY   RIO DE JANEIRO   BEIJING

Published in Nashville, Tennessee. Thomas Nelson is a registered trademark of Thomas Nelson, Inc.

Thomas Nelson, Inc., titles may be purchased in bulk for educational, business, fundraising, or sales promotional use. For information, please e-mail SpecialMarkets@ ThomasNelson.com.

Published in association with the literary agency of Sanford Communications, Inc., now part of Credo Communications LLC, www.credocommunications.net

Scripture quotations marked HCSB are taken from the *Holman Christian Standard Bible* (HCSB). © 1999, 2000, 2002, 2003 by Holman Bible Publishers, Nashville, Tennessee. All rights reserved.

Scripture quotations marked NIV are taken from the HOLY BIBLE: NEW INTERNATIONAL VERSION®. © 1973, 1978, 1984 by International Bible Society. Used by permission of Zondervan Publishing House. All rights reserved.

Library of Congress Cataloging-in-Publication Data

Burgess, Rick.
    Rick and Bubba's guide to the almost nearly perfect marriage / by Rick Burgess and Bill "Bubba" Bussey ; with Martha Bolton.
        p. cm.
    Includes bibliographical references and index.
    ISBN 978-1-4016-0399-1 (trade paper)
    1. Marriage—Humor. I. Bussey, Bubba. II. Bolton, Martha, 1951– III. Title.
PN6231.M3B85 2009
818'.602—dc22   2009003580

Printed in the United States of America

09 10 11 12 13 HCI 5 4 3 2

Dedication

This book is dedicated to our wives,
Betty Bussey and Sherri Burgess.

*So the L*ORD *God caused a deep sleep to come over the man, and he slept.
God took one of his ribs and closed the flesh at that place. Then the L*ORD
*God made the rib He had taken from the man into a woman and brought
her to the man. And the man said:*

> *This one, at last, is bone of my bone,
> and flesh of my flesh;
> this one will be called woman,
> for she was taken from man.
> This is why a man leaves his father and mother and bonds with
> his wife, and they become one flesh.*

—Genesis 2:21–24 HCSB

Contents

Introduction

Why would we, the two sexiest fat men in America, write a book on marriage? Well, for one thing, we both strongly believe in the institution of marriage. Also, between us we have survived more than thirty-three years of marriage, so we can speak from experience.

Our marriages aren't perfect. We've made our share of mistakes; our wives have made their share of mistakes. That is why the title of this book is *Rick and Bubba's Guide to the Almost Nearly Perfect Marriage*. If we had all the answers, it would be *Rick and Bubba's Guide to the Perfect Marriage*.

But our marriages *are* almost nearly perfect. So we figured that qualifies us to write a book on marriage. After all, no author can claim to have the perfect marriage. Why? Because the perfect marriage doesn't exist. It doesn't exist because *perfect people don't exist.* Prince Charming shows up only in fairy tales; and if we're honest with ourselves, the Stepford Wives were a little creepy.

The way we see it is this: marriage wasn't meant to be perfect. It was to teach us how to love an imperfect person perfectly. But before you start nodding at that "imperfect" description of your spouse, you need to know that it cuts both ways. Your spouse has to learn to love your flawed self too.

Marriage is a journey of growth for both parties. But you have to pack well for the trip. Some of the things you'll need to take with you are love, patience, forgiveness, grace, determination, and a healthy sense of humor.

Why patience? Because your spouse will exasperate you from time to time. In fact, you can count on it.

Why forgiveness? Because, not being perfect, he or she will do things that will need to be forgiven. And whether you want to admit it or not, you will need that forgiveness just as often as your spouse needs yours.

Why grace? Because there will be times when your spouse flat out won't deserve to be forgiven. But in the same way that God gives us unmerited favor, you might need to extend grace to your spouse, too.

Pack a lot of determination for the journey, because you'll need it to stand strong in the face of life's storms. No marriage escapes its share of rough weather. If you don't have determination to endure whatever winds and waves come your way, you'll be jumping overboard at the first rock of the boat.

Take along a sense of humor. Laughter is like oil to the engine of a marriage. If you can laugh, you can keep it going for a whole lot of years to come.

Most important, you'll need love for the trip. Love is the reason you do all the other things. Never forget how important your love—and the demonstration of that love—is to your marriage. And remember that it's especially important to demonstrate your love whether you're feeling it at the moment or not.

In *Rick and Bubba's Guide to the Almost Nearly Perfect Marriage*, we share some of our imperfections (not all of them, of course; that would require a trilogy). We share laughable moments and plenty of good memories. And we impart our thoughts on marriage. As an added bonus, we have included the highly secret, closely guarded *Book of Blame*. Until now, only women have been privy to this book. Men learned about it first when their wives started quoting from it. But sparing no expense in the investigative process, we have uncovered a copy of this elusive tome and now share it with you, though you will need to promise confidentiality. If you can't make that kind of promise, then stop reading when you come to that section. You're on the honor system. Don't make our wives have to make us come looking for you.

The most important thing that we hope comes through the pages of this book is our overwhelming love for our wives. Without them, we'd be lost—we know that. And we confess it freely. Their presence in our lives has been more than we could have hoped for.

Our goal in writing this book is that you'll start looking at your own marriage with new eyes. Appreciate what you've got. Don't waste precious years wishing that your mate were perfect. He or she is never going to be perfect. And anyway, it gives you something in common—your spouse isn't married to a perfect mate either.

One way to slow down the rising rate of divorce is for each of us to take an honest inventory of our own imperfections, and then thank the good Lord in heaven every day that our spouse puts up with us. We do this, and believe us, when we get through with the inventory, we're ready to do whatever chores our wives have in mind.

So whether you're happily married, unhappily married, engaged and hoping, or single and looking, we hope this book provides you with the kind of insight into matrimony you're not likely to get anywhere else. In fact, we can almost guarantee that.

We're not marriage counselors, family therapists, or Dr. Phil. I (Rick) am a licensed minister and can legally marry and bury you, but beyond giving our experiences and opinions on married life, as well as pointing you to what God says on the subject, that's about all we can offer.

Hopefully, though, this book will make you laugh, think, and appreciate a little more that person you promised to love.

First Impressions

When Betty and I (Bubba) first met, I was a lot thinner than I am right now. (Or maybe I was taller.) I was in high school, eighteen years old, and weighed in at around 170 pounds. I was a little harder on the scale by the time I got to college. I had shot up to about 210 pounds. And the scale hasn't stopped spinning since. Back then, though, I was in pretty good shape. In fact, I was quite the catch. At least that's what I wrote in Betty's yearbook.

Oh, and did I mention I also had permed hair? Betty claims that it was my permed hair that kept her attention off any weight issues I may have had. "I couldn't get past that perm," Betty confessed on our radio show one day not too long ago. I believe the exact words she used to describe it were "that goofy perm."

Goofy perm? And here, all these years, I thought it looked kind of cool, in an electrocuted Tom Jones kind of way.

Isn't that just like a woman, though? We men, as insecure as most of us are already, go out of our way to try to look appealing to our wives. But it seems like the harder we try, the more they laugh at us. Am I right, guys? We tried platform shoes, Nehru jackets, and Elvis hair and sideburns. All we got were snickers, giggles, and belly laughs.

Sorry . . . Betty has just commandeered the computer for her version of the story:

1

"I remember the first day I met Bill 'Bubba' Bussey. Of course, he wasn't 'Bubba' back then. He was just 'Bill.'

"Bill drove up in this gold 280Z, with speakers that were as big as the car. He had 12-inch woofers pointing up, three-way 6 x 9s pointing forward, with a crossover network. Let's just say, you could hear him coming. The ground would start vibrating from a block away.

"Bill was cool. He looked over at me like he really had something going on. But I couldn't react. I was too busy trying not to lose my cookies from the vibration in my chest caused by those speakers. So while I was trying my best not to get sick, he was trying his best to look cool and catch my attention.

"He did catch it, though. And as they say, the rest is history."

(Me again—Bubba—and I still say, she really did like that perm.)

Catching Your Mate

This chapter is for any single guys who may be reading this book. If you're reading it, either you're looking for advice on marriage for when you take the plunge into matrimony, or you're trying to figure out what might have gone wrong in your last relationship and how not to repeat those same mistakes.

We're glad you've come to the right source.

Many of today's young men are lost when it comes to the fine art of dating. Frankly, they are way too passive and need to get more aggressive in their search for the right woman. I (Rick) watch these young guys, and it's as if they think that the woman that God intends for them to marry is just going to happen along. Unless she's the Avon lady, it's highly unlikely that she's going to show up on your doorstep.

If the two of us had just waited around for Sherri and Betty to finally decide to marry us, we would probably be living like the Odd Couple, and we're not sure which one of us would be Felix.

Men, when it comes to finding the right mate, you have to be determined and focused. And not give up too soon. We walked right up to the line of stalking these two beautiful women. We didn't cross the line, of course; we stopped before they had legal grounds to keep us away.

But we never gave up.

I (Rick) played the world-famous friend approach in order to get myself into Sherri's company, and then I sort of worked my way from there. I would often talk to her about what losers other men were and how she shouldn't be treated that way. This, of course, implied how I would treat her like a queen if she would just give me the chance.

When I got up the courage, I began to get a little bolder and told her exactly how I felt and that my intentions were to marry her one day. (Sherri claims that if you look at our wedding pictures today, there is a look on my face that says, "Hey, look, I pulled this off just as planned.")

So my confidence played in my favor. Women love confidence in a man, but that's not to be confused with cockiness or arrogance.

Women also love it when a guy seems interested in what is important to them. Guys, when you're out with a woman, ask her about herself, take interest in who she is and what she likes, believes, wants, needs, expects, and dreams about. Get to know the real her; that'll go a long way toward getting her interested in knowing more about you.

And all of you single ladies out there, don't get lured into the "I will not settle" lie. If my wife had not settled for imperfection, we wouldn't be married today. I assure you that when she was a little girl, I was not what she was thinking her Prince Charming would turn out to be. For one thing, I couldn't even get the tights over my knees. I was older, already had a couple of kids, and had plenty of baggage.

But I can also assure you that we could not be happier. The way I treat her and the way I attempt to honor her are much more important than how tight my abs may or may not be or any mistakes I may have made in my past.

So don't look for perfection. Chances are pretty good that you're not without flaws either. None of us are. Find someone whose imperfections you can live with, and he yours, and see if something develops. If you fall in love, put God at the center of your marriage and watch how everything else falls into place.

Rick and Bubba's Surefire Ways for Guys to Know She's the One

For those of you who haven't taken the plunge into matrimony yet, we thought it would be good to give you some tips to know whether the girl you're considering marrying is the right one for you.

You'll know she's the right one if . . .

- ♥ she believes the "triple option offense" is the greatest offense ever created in football, and she thinks the "spread offense" is ruining the game.
- ♥ she knows everything there is to know about you and still wants to be in the same room.
- ♥ she will prepare wild game for dinner and never once flinch.
- ♥ she encourages you to go off more often with your guy friends to hunt and fish.
- ♥ she loves red meat.
- ♥ she says, "I just don't think men should change diapers."
- ♥ she has her own bass boat.

- ❤ she loves to cut grass.
- ❤ she enjoys cleaning house and doesn't want anyone else to do it.
- ❤ she hates soccer and doesn't want her sons playing it.

Ball and Chain?

A misconception held by many single men and women is that they have more freedom than do married people. Nothing could be further from the truth.

Yet singles will brag that by staying unattached, they don't have to answer to a spouse and they have the freedom to come and go as they please. They will even go so far as to describe a married relationship as "the old ball and chain."

We challenge that notion and will here prove its inaccuracy once and for all. Married people are not the ones who wear a ball and chain. The shackled ones are single guys in unhealthy relationships.

Exhibit One: Whenever we're with our single friends, we don't spend near the amount of time on the cell phone with our significant other as they do. They are the ones with the receiver pressed to their ear and so deep in conversation that they tune out everyone else. We don't know what they're talking about, but there's a lot of uh-huhing going on: "Uh-huh, uh-huh, uh-huh, I'm sorry, uh-huh, uh-huh. Pleeeeeeease, can I . . . uh-huh, uh-huh. Oh, all right, I'll be right there, sweetie."

So who's the one dragging around the ball and chain?

Wives are much more secure than that. If a married man calls his wife to check in or to tell her he's going to be late, the conversation will usually go something like this, "Hi, hon. I'm gonna stop by _____ (*fill in whatever store*). See you in a bit. Love ya. Bye."

We don't have to beg or plead or apologize for the extra time it's going to take. The call is merely a heads-up, a courtesy call, just to let her know that we'll be a little late.

When the guy with a girlfriend calls to say he's going to be late for their dinner date, he barely gets the words out before his date's voice starts blasting through the phone line, in a pitch of whine never before heard on this earth. Never mind the fact that she has just spent the previous hour text messaging him; never mind that this is her third phone call in the same amount of time; never mind that the Goodyear blimp flying overhead is scrolling the words "You're late!" The guy will still insist that because he's single, he has his freedom. He'll even say something ridiculous after he hangs up, like, "You know, I'd get married, but I just enjoy my independence too much. Hey, look, is that the Goodyear blimp? Slow down so I can read what it says . . . Well, lookie there. She loves me!"

It's pathetic.

We husbands and wives have a mutual understanding that we'll tell each other what we're going to be doing so that the other person can go ahead and make plans. It's not a ball and chain; it's called *communication*. That way no one's waiting at home with dinner on the table getting cold or having to wonder who, if anybody, picked up the kids. A married couple operates as a team, and when the team is running smoothly, it's a beautiful thing.

Exhibit Two: Most of us married men can do anything we want to . . . as long as we take the kids. We can golf, go bowling, sky-dive, go to the sporting goods store—the only catch is, we've got to load up the kids and take them with us. Most wives don't care where you go, as long as you're hauling around the offspring.

Our single friends think this is a ploy by our wives to make sure we get home on time. But it's not. They just enjoy knowing that the kids are spending time with their dad. And since we enjoy the company of our children, it works out for everyone.

Exhibit Three: When we take our really fine wives out for the evening we can continue the date when we get back home without worrying about going against God. That's real freedom. Despite what many—even in the church—overlook today, it is still against the teachings of the Bible to live together before marriage.

But after a date night with your wife, you can go home and sleep together and not feel one bit of guilt. When we get that "special" look from our wives over a fried shrimp platter at Denny's, we don't have to wrestle over what happens later that evening. If she has loving on her mind, all we have to do is say, "Oh, really? *Well, all right!*"

When I (Bubba) get that "special" look from Betty, it usually means something different. Betty's "come hither" look just means we're having spaghetti. *"You've got that twinkle in your eye again, babe. And I know what that means. Italian!"*

To be fair, Betty says my own sexy look leaves a lot to be desired too. She says it makes me look like my tummy hurts. I'll give her what I think is a romantic look from across the table, and she'll just say, "Honey, you okay? You got gas again? We've talked about what Mexican food does to you."

I guess I still need to work on "my look."

So there you have it—proof positive that guys with girlfriends, or gals with boyfriends, actually have less freedom than those of us who are happily married. Stay single if you want, but don't do it because of the freedom you think you'll be losing if you say, "I do." The wedding vows aren't a ball and chain; they're a promise to mutually love, respect, and honor each other. If that sounds good to you, if it sounds better than what you've experienced so far in your single life, then jump on in; the water's fine.

Rules of Engagement for Women

1. Your husband-to-be is currently acting like he is fourteen years old. This is not going to change. You might want to lower your expectations to a goal of his maturing to age twenty-one after you have been married for, say, twenty more years.

2. If your husband-to-be loves to watch sports, and he also seems to hunt and fish a lot while you're dating, assume that he will still have those desires when he is your husband.

3. Men are not complicated. Feed your man, and be excited about intimacy between a husband and a wife, and he will be very happy and contented all the days of his life.

4. Men do not care at all about how the house will be decorated. Please don't ask them about curtains, bedspreads, china, paint colors, or, and most especially, duvets (whatever those are).

5. Men do care about the electronics in the house. Don't ever freelance in choosing these. Include your fiancé in every purchase, or just let him go get that stuff himself.

6. Never tell your fiancé that you don't want a present for special occasions. He will think you mean it and continue the practice throughout your marriage.

7. If you don't care what dress your sweetheart likes better on you, don't ever put him in the position of picking one out for you. Work this out for yourself.

8. All shoes are the same to a man. Don't even ask.

9. Never buy your husband clothes for a gift— unless the clothes are for you and they have romance as a theme.

10. Men will take alone time with you over any gift, so give it to them generously (unless, of course, it's alone time to discuss long-term-future plans; remember, men live in the now).

Rules of Engagement for Men

1. Women make their rules up as they go.

2. Unlike a man, who never changes quickly enough for a woman, your wife will change

into many different women throughout your marriage.

3. Despite what they're telling you, women do care where and what they eat.

4. Despite what they're telling you, women do want a gift.

5. Despite what they're telling you, women really do want you to ask them what they like and how their day went. But before you do, make sure you have plenty of time on hand and a place to sit.

6. Tell her how beautiful she is every single day.

7. Teach her to love wild game, and your sporting life will go much easier.

8. Say good-bye to your single guy friends. They cause nothing but trouble.

9. Do not buy anything that helps with housework for a gift.

10. Add 30 percent to whatever line item is in the budget that involves both her and a checkbook or debit card.

Kiss and Tell

One of the reasons we married our wives is that they are good kissers. It's not the main reason, but it certainly is near the top of the list.

Kissing is important in a marriage. It's a romantic expression of love, and depending on the flavor of lipstick, it tastes good. I (Rick) don't think I could have married a bad kisser. I really don't. If everything else were perfect—great personality, good looks, a compatible belief system, and a great sense of humor—if she had all those qualities but was a bad kisser, I think we would have had problems.

Luckily, I didn't have to struggle over that issue with Sherri. She's a great kisser. I still remember our first kiss. It was an accidental one. Well, sort of. I couldn't hear what she was saying, so she leaned down to get closer, and she got right up on my cheek. So I did the only thing I could do—the classic turnover move. This is where you sort of turn your cheek so that your lips can't help but meet. The next thing I knew, it was contact, and then . . . *wow!* I don't mean to brag on my wife as an amazing kisser . . . okay, I do mean to brag. Sherri is an amazing kisser!

Now that I've had a paragraph to think about it, if Sherri hadn't been a good kisser, I still would have kept on dating her. She was the most beautiful girl I had ever met and was off the chart in every other way, too. So if she had been a bad kisser, I probably would have told her we needed to put in some extra time working on our technique— practice kissing sessions to perfect our skills. I don't think she would have minded.

After all, kissing is an art. There's a lot more to it than you think. First, the docking has to be just right. You can't simply go at each other's lips willy-nilly. The tilt and the lockup have to be right-on. They have to match up as perfectly as possible because the lips need to have a good seal. If you miss a few centimeters on the docking, or if you're off on your tilt in the slightest way, you'll forfeit the lockup and lose the seal. It's all scientific.

Kissing can also be tricky if you're an allergy sufferer like me (Bubba). You have to time your breathing to go with the kiss. Breathe, wheeze, kiss. Breathe, wheeze, kiss. Trust me, it's a lot more romantic than it sounds. (Of course, you can kiss and not breathe, but I wouldn't rec- ommend it. You might pass out and then your date will eat all your popcorn.)

All in all, the way we see it is this: kissing is a lot like ice cream. The worst we've ever had was still pretty good.

Rick and Bubba Unravel the Mystery of the "Marriage Vows"

We believe fewer marriages would end up in divorce court if only couples knew what it is they're promising when they say, "I do." So we are going to try to paint a clearer picture of what the marriage vows really mean. This way, if you're considering marriage, you won't be able to say that no one warned you. And if you're already married, it'll serve as a reminder of what you've promised.

For Better:	For Worse:
She cooks a delicious dinner.	She burns down the kitchen every night.
He brings home flowers.	He brings home poison ivy.
She wins the Publishers Clearing House sweepstakes.	She overdraws the checking account.
He leaves love notes hidden around the house.	He does the same with his dirty socks.

She's a huge fan of football and happens to love his favorite team.	She thinks the Super Bowl is a popcorn size at the movie theater.
He doesn't snore.	The Richter scale has picked him up four times.
She's fine with buying a new fishing boat.	—because she backed the car over the last one.
He helps clean up around the house.	He had to have skin grafts after his back stuck to the leather recliner.
She's frugal and accounts for every dime she spends.	She makes him do the same.
He bags a deer that supplies her with enough meat to last all winter.	He spends $4,328 on equipment and the hunting trip to do it.

In Sickness:

In Health:

He leads a sedentary lifestyle.	She buys his and hers treadmills.
He's forty pounds overweight.	She goes on a diet and removes every food item that contains calories from the house.
He falls victim to the Ebola virus.	She falls victim to a gym equipment auction on eBay.

She endures seventeen hours of labor, followed by an emergency cesarean section.	He wishes he could get pampered at the hospital like that.
He gets the flu.	She gets a tan. (See page 137, "Is There a Helpmate in the House?")
She passes out on the Little League field. (See page 137, "Is There a Helpmate in the House?")	She signs you both up for tennis lessons.
He injures himself in a fireworks display gone bad.	He breaks the long distance record running from the explosion.
She has a credit card addiction.	He uses the credit cards for target practice.
He becomes delusional about his college football career.	She helps him back to reality but bronzes his football jersey anyway.
He gets a mullet haircut.	He publicly repents for the existing mullet and burns all photos.

And then, of course, there's the "forsaking all others" part of the marriage vows. But what does "forsaking all others" mean? A lot more than we think it does.

Forsaking All Others:

- Forsaking watching soap operas and negatively comparing your husband to the better-looking lead character.

- Forsaking the discussion of your marital issues with any member of the opposite sex through e-mails, over lunch, at work, or through other encounters. That's what marriage counselors are for.

- Forsaking those who jump on the bandwagon during your marital troubles and who, for their own selfish reasons, may add fuel to your frustration instead of trying to help heal your marriage.

- Forsaking cell phone calls during your date nights.

- Forsaking friends who encourage or support you in an outside relationship during a time of separation from your spouse.

- Forsaking the boat salesman who tries to talk you into a new boat when you're behind on your house payment.

- Forsaking the hairstylist who gossips with you about your marriage.

- Forsaking the flippant use of the threat of divorce during minor disagreements.

- Forsaking the Internet when your spouse is trying to communicate.

- Forsaking a hunting trip when your wife—okay, let's not get carried away.

And how long is this promise for? Well, we can tell you that it's *not*:

- until someone better looking comes along
- until someone with a more secure future comes along

- until someone in better shape comes along
- until someone your family approves of comes along
- until someone your friends like better comes along
- until someone more grateful comes along
- until someone who won't nag comes along
- until someone funnier comes along
- until someone more interesting comes along
- until someone with a better personality comes along
- until someone more mature comes along
- until someone younger comes along
- until someone healthier comes along
- until someone richer comes along
- until someone more exciting comes along

God never intended marriage to be a trade-in, trade up, bailout, or "I'm outta here" proposition. Some marriages ultimately don't work out, but don't you think you still owe it to yourself, to your spouse, to your children, and to God to seek counseling before giving up on that person you loved enough to marry in the first place?

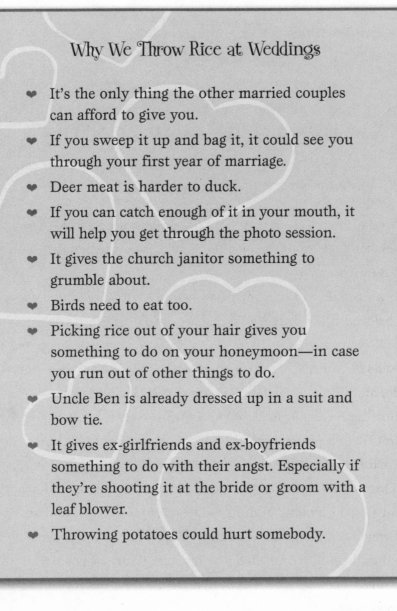

Why We Throw Rice at Weddings

- It's the only thing the other married couples can afford to give you.

- If you sweep it up and bag it, it could see you through your first year of marriage.

- Deer meat is harder to duck.

- If you can catch enough of it in your mouth, it will help you get through the photo session.

- It gives the church janitor something to grumble about.

- Birds need to eat too.

- Picking rice out of your hair gives you something to do on your honeymoon—in case you run out of other things to do.

- Uncle Ben is already dressed up in a suit and bow tie.

- It gives ex-girlfriends and ex-boyfriends something to do with their angst. Especially if they're shooting it at the bride or groom with a leaf blower.

- Throwing potatoes could hurt somebody.

Love and Debit Cards

No matter how long I live, I (Rick) will never forget my honeymoon with Sherri. This may not sound all that unusual. Most people remember their honeymoons, but I guarantee you it's for completely different reasons.

It all began with my trying to plan a memorable honeymoon for my beloved bride. I figured a cruise would be perfect because it was one all-inclusive fee and I wouldn't have to worry about money once we set sail. We could eat, see the shows, do whatever else we wanted to do, and I'd never have to take my wallet out of my pocket.

But the best-laid plans of mice and newlyweds often go astray. I hadn't figured on the cash we might spend on our off-ship excursion to Cozumel, Mexico.

This is where things get a little fuzzy. Even though I knew there might soon be trouble in Burgess Debit Land, we still went ahead and had way too much fun in Cozumel. Way, way too much fun.

I didn't think too much about my new financial position until the next morning when an announcement came over the ship's public address system.

"The ship needs to see the following people: Rick Burgess . . ."

More names were called, but I didn't hear anyone's name past mine. I wasn't sure what the problem was, but headed off to the ship's accounting offices.

"Are you Mr. Rickkkk Brrrrgiz?" a man asked, in a Norwegian accent that sounded more like German.

I looked out the porthole and could see Cuba in the distance. We were in international waters. I didn't know what laws we were under out there, so I weighed my words very carefully.

"Yes, that's me." *What'd I say that for?* I thought. So I rephrased it.

"I mean, what if I'm not him, but I'm speaking on his behalf?"

His eyes narrowed. "Mr. Burrrrgiz, ze credit card that you gave to us sez you have only $230. But you already owe us around one thouzand."

"Well, then," I said. "It looks like we've got a problem."

"Vat iz this Campus Bank?"

"That's a bank in Alabama."

"Alabama?"

I dropped a few names of famous Alabamians, thinking that might help. But it didn't. I even told him that my dad was a coach at Jackson State. That didn't help either. I was grasping at straws. I tried to think of famous Norwegians so I could drop a few of their names, but I couldn't think of any famous Norwegians.

The only name that seemed to register with him was American Express. And that didn't sound all that Norwegian. It didn't matter, because I didn't have one of their cards either.

At that point it was clear that our honeymoon was going south fast. I didn't know if I was going to get thrown off the boat or have to work kitchen duty at the midnight buffet.

Meanwhile, Sherri still had no idea what the announcement had been about. She was my new bride and wasn't yet privy to my financial planning skills, so she figured everything was fine and that the announcement had been about some special show tickets that I had ordered or something.

Back in Alabama, everyone I knew had received at least one panicked phone call from me asking—make that *pleading*—for help. And money. I tried to call Bubba, but I couldn't reach him. (He seems to have a supernatural awareness of these sorts of things and knows when to be out of cell phone range. He says it's a gift.)

The trip to the ship's accountant's office now became a daily excursion for me. But to no avail. Being at sea, there wasn't anything I could do to fix the situation myself, so after a while, I just started ignoring the PA announcements. It had become painfully apparent that I wasn't going to have any money in my account until after we docked, and there wasn't anything anyone could do about it. So I did what I always do in situations like this—I went into what I call the Burgess "Kill Me" stage. This is the stage when I reach the point where I just don't care. It's kind of like a release valve—a way to let off pressure when I've had all I can take. And I had definitely reached that stage on that ship. I was at the *Hey, do whatever you've got to do. Throw us off the ship if you have to. I don't care* point.

I had been disrupting everyone's life by asking them to get money into my account. I'd heard that Speedy, our right arm at the radio station, had been on the phone with my family, and I knew that everybody's life was being interrupted for my lack of planning. So I decided to go back to the ship's accountant and level with him.

"Look," I said, "I'm on my honeymoon and I'm tired of worrying about all of this. I'll have the money after we dock. That's the best I can do."

"Ve vill check with this Compass bank to see if you have zee money," he said.

"The money is not going to be there," I said. "It won't be in my account until we are off the ship in Miami, and maybe not until a few days later. And it's *Campus* Bank."

The guy stared at me and then gave me a sarcastic, smug smile. "Ve vill take it up with your bank," he repeated. "You can go now."

Now, most people would feel pretty lucky at that point to not be thrown overboard. They would have thanked him and then gone back to their cabin to spend the rest of the cruise eating crackers and whatever M&M's they could find behind the sofa.

Not me. The way I saw it, I had just been given a reprieve. If they were going to wait for their money, which I really was going to have, it was party time!

Of course, from then on, every time they read a list of names over the loudspeaker, Sherri and I would pause briefly for a moment of silence before going on about our business. And the other passengers did start looking at us with a funny tilt to their heads, as if to say, "Hey, aren't you that couple who keeps getting called to the captain's office?" It could have been our imagination, but it seemed whenever we walked into a room, people would scatter away from us. Maybe they were afraid we were going to ask them for a bailout.

Speaking of captains, can anyone tell me why the captain attends all these gala dinners? Shouldn't he be driving the ship? What is he doing eating with the passengers when we could be headed straight for an iceberg?

I don't care how dressed up he gets, or how hungry; I want the captain of any ship that I'm on to be eating in the control room! Can't someone take him a hamburger or something, and tell him to keep on steering the ship?

It all worked out, though. As soon as we got home from the cruise, I went to my bank and got my financial situation straightened out. All things considered, it was a great honeymoon. And no sign of an iceberg anywhere.

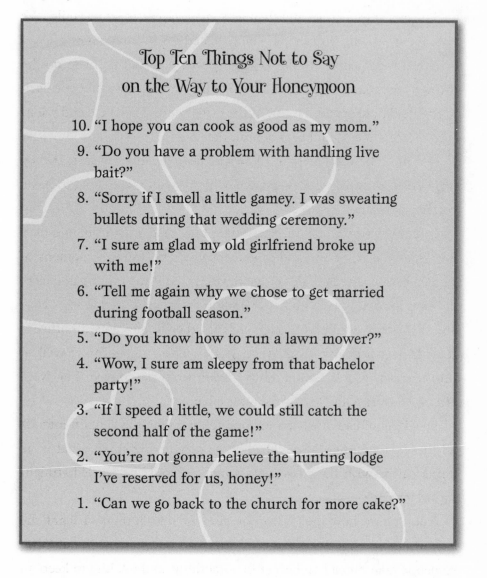

Top Ten Things Not to Say
on the Way to Your Honeymoon

10. "I hope you can cook as good as my mom."

9. "Do you have a problem with handling live bait?"

8. "Sorry if I smell a little gamey. I was sweating bullets during that wedding ceremony."

7. "I sure am glad my old girlfriend broke up with me!"

6. "Tell me again why we chose to get married during football season."

5. "Do you know how to run a lawn mower?"

4. "Wow, I sure am sleepy from that bachelor party!"

3. "If I speed a little, we could still catch the second half of the game!"

2. "You're not gonna believe the hunting lodge I've reserved for us, honey!"

1. "Can we go back to the church for more cake?"

To Love, Honor, and . . . Duck!

According to a certain tabloid that shall remain nameless, a Swiss psychiatrist has suggested that a woman should get rid of her pent-up frustrations by slapping her husband at least once a day when he least expects it. I'm sorry, but we take issue with this. For one thing, this would never be accepted as a valid solution for a man's pent-up frustrations. So why should it ever be considered acceptable behavior for a woman?

According to the tabloid, though, after several weeks of slapping her man every day, a woman in the study had successfully rid herself of all her frustrations. She allegedly said that after the daily slap, her husband began respecting her more, and she regained her sense of self-worth.

On the other hand, her poor husband probably didn't have any self-worth, or teeth, left.

We are so glad that our wives have never resorted to this kind of physical assault on us. The worst thing I (Bubba) had to do was dodge a flying glass that had been thrown in my direction during our third year of marriage. It didn't hit me, but unfortunately for Betty, she was soon to discover that I was a much better thrower than she was. And I now had the glass.

To show my respect, and to even up the score, I pitched the glass back to her. But it was a soft pitch tossed low and wide to serve only as a warning. I wanted to let her know that I could play along with her little game, if she really wanted me to.

So what was it that had caused such an upheaval in our relationship that we would both resort to this kind of adolescent behavior?

All I remember is that a few days before the incident, Betty had asked me about planting some new flowers in the flower bed because our summer flowers had died. I figured replacement flowers would cost about eighty bucks, and since we had been trying to save up for a dining room set, I thought the flowers could wait. The dining room set was our big project that we both had agreed on, and eighty bucks would go a long way toward purchasing it. It could at least be the down payment. So after presenting my position, we agreed not to get flowers. The key word is *agreed.*

A few days later, I drove up to our house and what did I see? The prettiest new carpet of flowers you can imagine, already planted in our front yard, stretching on as far as the eye could see.

When I parked and got out of the car, I said, "Betty, I thought we weren't going to get new flowers."

She said, "No, we agreed to get the flowers. Don't you remember?"

And there it was. Betty had played the crazy card. The crazy card is when your wife remembers something totally different from the way you remember it. Your story differs from hers; therefore, you are crazy.

But this time the crazy card wasn't going to work. I was positive that she had been in agreement with me.

Still, that incident wasn't as bad as the time when we had agreed not to buy furniture for the new house until it was built. But then one day Betty showed up with a truck full of it! That one cut me to my decorative core. Not only had she once again gone against what we had both agreed on, but she had totally left me out of the furniture selection process. Why is it that women assume we men don't have any opinions when it comes to selecting furniture, pillows, or our kids' names? (We don't, of course—refer back to Rules of Engagement for Women, rule 4—but we still want you to pretend to include us!) Sure, sometimes you women will ask us for our opinions, but that's about as far as it goes. In some marriages, the wife will even purposely make selections that she knows good and well her husband doesn't want. It's a power play, and it's also why we have children walking around today named Wisteria and StarShadow.

My (Rick's) wife, Sherri, has never thrown a glass in my direction, but she did dump a bucket of ice on top of me once. I don't even remember what the disagreement was about. But I do recall it was in the early years of our marriage.

Now, you've got to get this visual. I am six foot two, 270 pounds, and my wife, Sherri, is five feet tall. When she's not pregnant, she's probably all of about 115 pounds. But when she's mad, she looks a lot taller. Especially that day when I was sitting at the kitchen table and she approached me from behind.

But there I was, trying to "lay down the law" on some newlywed spat, and the next thing I knew, a bucket of cold ice was dumped over my head and falling down my shirtless back.

My first reaction was to completely dismantle the kitchen. But a cooler head prevailed (thanks to the ice), and I managed to keep control. The argument was silly, anyway. No one is a bigger smart aleck than I am, and I had "smart-alecked" myself right into a bit of a frenzy. Sherri had no choice but to let loose with the ice. (Okay, she did have a choice. But I probably had the ice shower coming.)

But even Bubba's glass or my bucket of ice doesn't hold a candle to what happened to one of the guys we work with at the radio station. His wife once poured an entire bottle of ranch dressing on him. It seems his wife and he were at a restaurant when a disagreement over their order erupted, and she had apparently reached the "Enough!" level on the Marriage Warning System and said, "Well, here! You can just have it!" Then she dumped the entire bottle of dressing on him.

So with all due respect to the Swiss psychiatrist, we don't agree with the notion of slapping your husband daily. Throwing glasses, dumping ice, or pouring ranch dressing on us probably aren't the best ways to communicate either. These kinds of things won't help a marriage. In fact, they'll more than likely hurt it. But you learn these things over time.

If you simply must throw something at us, make it a few scoops of ice cream. And pitch them low and wide. It's a much more loving thing to do.

Lost!

For years women have teased men about their unwillingness to stop and ask directions. They've cracked jokes that have made sport of how we will drive around for hours lost, rather than pull over and get out the map. We have listened to this ridicule and have not said much. We've let women rant on and on about how stubborn we can get when we're behind the wheel. But now it's time we spoke up in our defense. In writing this book about marriage, Article XI of the *Book of Blame* needs to be addressed.

A more detailed description of Article XI can be found in the back of this book, but the essence of it is this: When it comes to driving, women get just as lost as men.

Allow me (Rick) to prove our point by recounting the following story. Before I begin, I would like to note that Sherri is an amazing woman, but she has got to be the most headstrong person I know. Headstrong is a good quality when she's defending me or one of the kids. She won't take anything from anyone when it comes to protecting her family. But this quality can also cause a few problems in other areas of our lives—like it did on this one particular day when Bubba and I arranged for our wives to meet us at a certain location. Sherri had seemed to understand the directions, so we figured all would go well.

Silly us.

When Bubba and I arrived at the location, we realized that the place was a little trickier to find than what the directions had indicated. If you're not paying close attention, the building sort of sneaks up on you; so we thought we should call the girls (who were still en route) and give them a heads-up.

Since Sherri was driving the car and Betty was the passenger, it fell to me to be the one to make the call to my beloved.

"Hello, Sherri—" I said.

But for some reason Sherri was already on the defensive. All I was trying to do was give her a landmark to watch out for, but she seemed a little irritated. Being the loving husband that I am, I still tried to help her out even though I was sure I didn't deserve her slightly irritated tone of voice.

Since Bubba had suggested using the elementary school as a landmark, I went with it. It seemed like the perfect place to meet up. There were school buses lined up, a flagpole, big buildings. There was no way Sherri and Betty could miss that.

But Sherri didn't let me get the words out. Instead, she was apparently annoyed over the fact that I had even called. Sure, this was the *fourth* call and the *fourth* landmark that I had suggested, but still.

Sherri said that since she was taking care of small children, as well as driving, she was quite certain she could manage to find the location without my intervention. One thing I forgot to mention is that when Sherri gets focused on what she's doing, she really doesn't like to be bothered.

So I stated my defense.

"Hey, I just wanted you to know that there is another landmark that you could watch out for. I'm telling you, Sherri, the place where we're going today can really sneak up on you. For some reason, the sign is turned around parallel with the road, instead of being positioned horizontally where you can see it."

I was only trying to be helpful.

"Listen to me, Sherri," I continued. "Just look for an elementary school as soon as you get off Highway 119 and get on Highway 31. It's not far. It comes up pretty quick."

"Okay, Rick," she snarled. Then she hung up. I didn't buy into her frustration because I knew once she got there she would understand what I was talking about.

Figuring she was getting close, I decided to go stand in the parking lot and wait for her there. That would give her one more landmark to watch for—me. And I'm almost as hard to miss as a building.

After a while, with no sign of Sherri, I called her again.

"Where are you?" I asked, concerned.

"I'm on Highway 119, so that's not very far away."

"Okay," I said. "Just don't miss it. Look for the elementary school. You'll see me right there in the parking lot. And there's also—" I tried to throw in a couple more landmarks, just to be on the safe side, but she considered it overkill.

"Rick, why do you keep calling?"

"Well, I don't want you to get lost."

"I'm not going to get lost!" she insisted, and then, I kid you not, as we were talking, I looked up and saw her driving right by me! She passed the elementary school *and* me, and continued on down the highway, still telling me on the phone how she wasn't going to get lost! My petite, beautiful, and otherwise law-abiding wife was doing about fifty miles an hour right through a school zone. All I saw was the blur of her blonde hair. She didn't even tap the brakes.

So I called her again.

"Hello, sweetie—"

"Rick!" she barked. "*Why do you keep calling?*"

I took the high road and didn't get into the whole "kill the messenger" speech that was going through my mind. I simply said, "Sherri, honey, you just passed it."

"No, I didn't."

"Sherri, I just saw you drive by us."

"Rick, I didn't pass it. I *know* where I'm going."

"Sherri, are you trying to say that I did not just see you drive past here? How long have you been on Highway 31? I'm telling you the place comes up immediately once you get on 31."

"Well, I haven't seen any school, so I haven't passed you."

"Sherri," I repeated, "I just saw you drive by."

Apparently she didn't like my confident tone of voice because of what happened next. I still can't believe it myself. *My beloved, otherwise patient and loving wife hung up on me!*

It was time for a traffic intervention. So I dialed her back, and she was, just as I expected, happy to hear my voice. She just hid it well.

"Rick, why do you keep calling?!" she yelled, which is our love language for, "Hi, honey. What's up?"

"Sherri, listen to me . . . please, for your own sake, *listen*. I'm calling because you are not here. You've missed the school! I'm trying to bring you back to me. Come home, Sherri! Come back to daddy, honey."

"Rick, I have not passed it!"

Then the phone went dead—again. I wasn't exactly sure what was going on with the reception in that area, so I called her—again.

And again.

And again.

Six calls later, I convinced her to turn around. I breathed a sigh of relief when I saw her coming again. Then I called her to direct her in.

"Here you are, Sherri. I see you. I see you! Keep coming."

Vrooommmm!

There she went!

It still took a few more calls to finally get Sherri to see us and pull into the school parking lot. But all's well that ends well, right?

Wrong.

Instead of jumping out of the car and wrapping her arms around me for saving her from driving around lost in a strange town into the wee hours of the night, she just got out and said, "Well, I'll tell you something, Rick Burgess. You give the worst directions I've ever heard!"

What? Did she really just say that? We were standing in the parking lot of the school that I had chosen as my landmark. The school was right where I said it would be. The flagpole was there, the buildings were there, the school buses were there. *How could she say it wasn't a good landmark?*

I tried to stay calm.

"Sherri, let's ponder this. Is it possible that you don't follow directions very well?"

I guess that hit some kind of nerve because after that we flew into a discussion of major proportions, right there in my landmark parking lot. Then I did what Sherri hates for me to do in the middle of a disagreement. I did the "arm around her" move. This is something I would highly recommend to all you husbands out there. Women have a difficult time telling you off when your arm is around them in a loving, tender embrace.

"Sherri, honey, let us gander at the elementary school standing here before us, which I told you numerous times to be looking for."

She didn't gander, but I could sense she was softening just a bit. She still had to get in the defense's closing statement, though.

"Boy, I tell you, that thing's way off the road, isn't it?" she said.

"I know, but maybe those Slow: School Zone signs could have been a hint that a school was near, you think? And look, they've even got a flashing light, too."

Okay, so at that point I was rubbing it in a bit. But it was an opportunity I couldn't let slide. I can't tell you how many times I have been the one in the wrong and have had to eat crow. So at long last, when it was finally my turn, when I was in the right for a change, I was going to enjoy it. This time I was 100 percent in the right. Sherri was going to have to admit that the reason she got lost had nothing to do with me. In fact, I had tried to warn her. I had given it my best shot, called her multiple times to help her out (in spite of her ridicule), but she still managed to get herself lost.

Yes, this was clearly a situation where the wife was to blame, and now she was going to have to apologize to me.

But every husband in the world knows what I had to eventually say.

"I'm so sorry, honey. It was all my fault."

And all was right with the world once again.*

* Refer to the *Book of Blame,* Article XI.

Annoying Habits

Okay, we'll confess it, ladies. We men do things that probably get on your nerves. We don't do them intentionally, but we still do them. One thing that I (Rick) know that gets on Sherri's nerves is when I make things harder than they need to be. Like when she asked me if I was ever going to trim my goatee.

"I would, honey," I said, "but my batteries are dead in my shaver."

"Well, put some new batteries in," she said. Sherri is so cute when she's logical.

"Naw . . . too much of a hassle," I said. I majored in illogic in high school.

Not putting new batteries in my shaver was bad enough, but then I called her a few days later on my way home from work and said, "Hey, honey, I'm going to be a little late. I'm going to stop off at the store and get a new shaver."

"You're going to buy another shaver instead of changing the batteries, Rick?"

"Well, that shaver's not working right. And besides, I don't know where it is."

I realize this is the kind of thinking that probably gets on Sherri's nerves. But again, it's my gift.

One thing that gets on my (Bubba's) wife's nerves is that I can never remember where I've put the household calculator; yet when it comes to my set of Craftsman tools, I can tell you exactly where the 5/8-inch open-end wrench is, and which wrench is currently in the holder. This, of course, annoys Betty to no end.

We're both reasonably sure that it also annoys our wives that we can get up at three o'clock in the morning to go hunting, but can't roll out of bed by ten o'clock to mow the lawn on our day off.

One of the most annoying things that many husbands do is to leave their clothes strewn all over the floor. Women do not understand our need for doing this. Let us try to explain. Ladies, this behavior dates back to the caveman, Renaissance, and Wild West days. It is our way of leaving a trail behind us so that we'll be able to find our way back should we ever get lost (and you already know how we hate to ask for directions). Men have been doing this sort of thing for centuries; you can't expect us to give it up now.

To be fair, women do annoying things, too. For one thing, what is it about women that requires so many electric hair products, and why must they all remain plugged in when not in use? Is this a trap you're setting for us? There's your curling iron, your hair-straightener, electric curlers, blow dryer, and who knows what else? There's hardly a plug left for your husband's shaver (when it's working) or his cell phone charger.

Another annoying thing that you women do is you try to change us. We've never understood this. Why do you marry us, and then suddenly want to change everything that seemed perfectly okay while we were dating? If you knew we watched a lot of sports before marriage, why do you think we would stop watching a lot of sports after marriage? If you knew we liked to go hunting or fishing or golfing before we married, what makes you think that we would suddenly lose our desire to do those things after marriage? Some things are part of our personality and can't be easily changed. Why make this a source of contention, especially if we didn't hide it from you during the courtship process?

And why in the world do you think you have to shake us awake when we're snoring? Can't you just whisper in our ear or do something a little less traumatic? You shake us out of a deep sleep and scare the living daylight out of us. No wonder our hair turns white sooner than yours!

The bottom line is, both husbands and wives do plenty of things that annoy each other. But if we look at our own annoying habits first, then our spouses' annoying habits might not seem so unbearable by comparison.

Why Is Our Stuff
the First to Go?

Whenever the economy is going through a rough place, the number of garage sales taking place on any given weekend seems to skyrocket. Have you noticed this? People start hauling out all those things they couldn't live without just a few short years (or months) ago and dragging them onto their front lawns to be sold to the highest bidder. Then they'll get one of their kids to post signs all over the neighborhood, announcing "Yard Sale," and it's "Let the games begin!"

Yard sales are an open invitation for people to rummage through your priceless souvenirs and the artifacts from your life, and offer you a dime for them.

Even so, garage sales can be a lot of fun. You get to meet the neighbors and carloads of total strangers, and you get to make a little money to boot.

You do need to prepare yourself for the feelings of rejection that are sure to come when someone decides to pass on your collection of 8-track tapes.

You should also prepare yourself for the early shoppers. Never mind that you have the starting time of 9 a.m. written on every sign, as well as in your newspaper ad. Garage sale shoppers are an early-rising bunch. They'll show up at your house long before your paperboy or the sun appears. Some shoppers might even park in front of your home the night before, and sleep there until morning just so they'll get first dibs on anything you drag out to your driveway. (If you play your cards right, you could make five bucks on your trash.)

The other thing you should prepare yourself for is the marital conflict that will most certainly arise during the yard sale. In fact, that's the reason we brought this subject up in a book on marriage in the first place. This seemingly harmless event has caused many a marital rift. What could possibly go wrong at a garage sale? *Everything!* But the main problem comes from this age-old question:

Why is the husband's stuff always the first to go?

"Honey, let's have a garage sale" is usually followed by an emotionless pricing of everything the husband holds near and dear to his heart. Yet when the same procedure is applied to a wife's things, then it's a Dr. Phil moment.

(Tearfully) *"I can't believe you're asking me to part with that. If you only knew what that means to me, you would never have asked such a thing, you beast!"*

So you toss the unicorn house slippers back into the closet and continue watching your loving wife cart all of your stuff to the curb.

I (Rick) hate garage sales. I don't care if you call them garage sales, yard sales, or rummage sales—I hate them all. I haven't talked to a therapist about this because I don't need to. I already know that my aversion to yard sales has to do with this lopsided sacrificing that goes on. Why are husbands asked to give up far more than wives?

Why is it that an item that has sat in the garage for the last seven years, an item that we just *had* to take with us to the new house even though we have never once used it, cannot *possibly* be considered for the yard sale? Like the juicer, all the exercise equipment, and yes, even a backwards fleece robe or two.

Who knows? But my old number 75 football jersey, my PETA shirt (People Eating Tasty Animals), my Tennessee Titans golf shirt, my lucky shirt (*every* wife knows good and well which one is her husband's favorite), my twelve-year-old jeans that still fit perfectly, and my satin radio station jacket are all on the rack for one dollar!

Also, I usually notice that quite a bit of my old hunting gear gets put out there on our driveway, too. Sure, I have bought four years' worth of replacements, but you never know when you might need a backup camo shirt or boots. And a backup for those backups. And a backup for the backup that's backing up the backups.

But does Sherri care?

No! Each item will be out there with a tag prominently dangling from it.

So once again, *why are these things for sale?* There is one reason and one reason only: *Because they belong to me!*

Wives don't understand that you cannot put a value on this kind of equipment. All they see as special is their grandmother's antique table. To them, our old recliners have no value. They don't see the stuffing popping out of the upholstery and think of it as artistic. They consider exploding upholstery a negative and will price the chair at about two bucks—if that. They won't even consider the slight tilt that it sits at to be beneficial for many back problems. They'll just want the chair to go to the highest bidder as quickly as possible.

Inequality, injustice, and unfairness—those are my reasons for not liking yard sales. I hate the whole helpless feeling I get when I realize that everything I have worked so hard to obtain is vanishing right before my eyes on a Saturday morning, and worse yet, it all goes for a combined total of five bucks! Do we really need five bucks that badly? Will five dollars make or break us? Will it make our house payment? Our car payment? Even one credit card payment?

No!

My recliner is worth more than five bucks. My camo shirt and boots are worth more than five bucks too. My jersey from the football season of 1982? Why, you can't even put a price on that! The sweat and blood that went into that jersey alone make it priceless! It really shouldn't even be out there. If she had to sell something of mine, where were the very uncomfortable button-downs that I had to wear when I worked in radio sales? She could sell those. I wouldn't care. And where are all the shirts that my precious wife thinks I will some-day be slim enough to wear again? Some dreams you just have to let go of, Sherri. *Let 'em go*, hon. But let me keep my jersey!

Wives, we're just asking you to be fair. That's all. It's our stuff. We've had it a long time. Don't ask us to part with it in such a cold and callous manner.

Either that or hold the yard sale when we're out of town. That way, at least the neighbors won't see us cry.

Three Sides to Every Story

Most people agree that there are always two sides to a story. But in marriage, we say there are *three* sides to a story. There's his side, there's her side, and then there's the truth. The truth may have elements of both sides, or it can be a far cry from either of the other two versions.

Here are some examples of what we mean:

The situation: The husband has just broken his ankle.
   His side: "I was going up to dunk the basketball in a pickup game, and I must have landed funny on it."
   Her side: "My husband refuses to act his age."
   The truth: He lost his balance on the way to get the mail, while talking to his buddy on the cell phone about the game.

The situation: The kids are not eating their dinner.
   His side: "I don't know . . . I guess they don't feel well or they just aren't hungry."
   Her side: "No one appreciates what I do around here!"
   The truth: Dad gave everyone ice cream on the way home after he picked them up from school.

The situation: The husband returns home with several bags of groceries, but almost nothing that his wife asked him to get is in them.

> *His side:* "What's up with the grocery store leaving out some of our stuff?"
>
> *Her side:* "You did not write down what I asked you to get, did you?"
>
> *The truth:* He did write it down, but then left it in the car and decided to trust his memory rather than going back to get it.

The situation: The family dog is missing.

> *His side:* "Hey, I think that serviceman left the gate open."
>
> *Her side:* "Oh, my gosh! Our dog has been pet-napped!"
>
> *The truth:* Everybody forgot that the dog is at the vet for shots and a bath.

The situation: "Great-looking outfit, dear. How much did it cost?"

> *His side:* "Who cares—as long as it leads to romance?"
>
> *Her side:* "It was on sale for only $63, marked down from $65, and I couldn't pass it up."
>
> *The truth:* Good-bye, new truck.

The situation: The husband comes home with new gear from the outdoors store.

> *His side:* "No, I just went in to look around, but then ol' Henry said I could try out this new equipment just to see if I like it."
>
> *Her side:* "He has just wasted our mortgage money on glorified toys—again."
>
> *The truth:* He has a secret account at the store.

The situation: The car ran out of gas.

His side: "Would it hurt you to put some gas in this thing once in a while?"

Her side: "You drove the car last. Why didn't you get it?"

The truth: You both decided you were too tired to get it last night and you agreed to get it later, when one of the older kids would be there to pump it.

The situation: The husband arrives home late.

His side: "There was an accident, and I got caught up in traffic."

Her side: "He was goofing off with the guys at work—again."

The truth: He took the long way home, via the hunting camp.

The situation: The phone bill is over $300.

His side: "You went over our minutes talking to your girlfriends!"

Her side: "You didn't bump up our minutes like I told you to, did you?"

The truth: Your four-year-old has been dialing Paris and ordering pizza.

The situation: The husband receives a parking ticket.

His side: "I'm fighting this! This is a legal parking space!"

Her side: "I told you not to park there. That's why they paint the curb red."

The truth: It's not even your car. Your car is across the street.

So there you have it. In any given argument, each side will have its own perspective. If you can acknowledge that the truth might be a combination of both sides, you'll go a long way toward bringing peace to your home.

The Ten Commandments of Marriage

1. Thou shalt not invite your buddies to the house to watch football but neglect to tell your wife about it until a few minutes before the caravan arrives.

2. Thou shalt apologize to your wife for whatever agony or discomfort she has had to endure on any given day, physically or emotionally, including mishaps with appliances or motor vehicles, or as a result of national or world events, because it is your fault. Accept it.

3. Dads, thou shalt not give your children ice cream for dinner. Giving it for breakfast is perfectly okay.

4. Wife, thou shalt never throw away your husband's high school football jersey, whether it still fits him or not.

5. Husband, thou shalt write down what your wife asked you to pick up on the way home from work, and thou shalt not freelance and pick up things you need yourself. Diverting from the list guarantees that you will forget one or more of her requested items.

6. Wife, thou shalt not lie about whether you want something for Mother's Day, birthdays, anniversaries, or Valentine's Day. If you tell us you're fine with not getting anything, *we'll believe you*. But if you really do want something, then tell us. If you want something specific, tell us specifically what that is. If you didn't get us anything, and you really don't want anything either, tell us. But if you really did get us something and are only saying you didn't, and then telling us not to get you anything, you forfeit your right to get upset with us if we don't have a gift. Men may not always do what they're told, but in these situations, we usually do. Tell us what you want, or don't want, and we'll do our best to get it. Or not get it. Get it?

7. Thou shalt love your spouse because you promised God that you would. Don't love your spouse for as long as he or she lives up to your standard. Love your spouse for as long as you promised God you would. Loving your spouse is an action, not a feeling.

8. As much as you love your spouse, thou shalt love God more. Then you will become the mate that God intended your spouse to have.

9. God made man and woman equal, but not the same. It's a fact of life. Thou shalt enjoy your

sameness and celebrate your differences. Some of those differences can be pretty nice.

10. Thou shalt never buy your wife a gift that is used for housework. (Yes, we've said it before, but trust us on this one—see Rules of Engagement for Men, #9.)

Why Couples Fight

Even after years of marriage, many couples still haven't mastered the fine art of fighting. We're not talking about the "get out the boxing gloves" kind of fighting. We're talking about all the debating, disagreeing, stating your case, arguing, or whatever-you-want-to-call-it kind of spats that come up from time to time in marriage.

Other than the obvious—don't get physical—the main thing to know about arguing with your spouse is that the fight is seldom about what it seems to be about on the surface. There is usually an underlying issue that runs much deeper. It is that underlying issue that you're really dealing with, or rather, *not* dealing with.

Here's what we mean:

What You Think the Fight's About: Which way the toilet paper roll is hung.

What It's Really About: Total control over all things bathroom. The bathroom, much like the kitchen, and the closet, and, well, the rest of the house, for that matter, is a woman's domain. A husband shouldn't even *think* of using the main bathroom in the house, especially if his wife is home at the time and awake.

Since the invention of indoor plumbing, men have been reduced to using the pitifully tiny guest bathroom of the house. If you don't think that's your designated place, take a look around the smaller bathroom.

You will find your shaver, your deodorant, and your toothbrush strategically placed in some out-of-the-way place there. Now go look in the main bathroom. You will not find a single thing belonging to you. Even the toilet in there will be one that you have never personally sat upon. That is your wife's toilet.

Don't even think about using it. You are only to use the one in the guest bathroom, or at the gas station, before coming home.

If you need more convincing, then take a look around at the shower curtain and window treatments in the master bathroom and ask yourself: "Would I have ever bought those if it were *my* bathroom? Would I have bought a floral toilet paper dispenser? Would I have a basket of paper napkins instead of a hand towel?"

We rest our case.

What You Think It's About: Where to eat.

What It's Really About: This is an easy one. It's obviously about that one question on every wife's mind 24/7: *Do you think I'm fat?* You'd be surprised how many marital arguments have this one question at their root.

Men, if your wife asks where you would like to eat, do not—we repeat, *do not*—answer this question. *It is a trap!* Whatever you do, keep your mouth closed and let *her* select the restaurant. If she suggests a nice Italian eatery, tell her that you'd absolutely *love* spaghetti. If she suggests Mexican, tell her you can already taste the tacos. If she says she feels like a burger, head straight to the best burger place in town. Do not pass "Go"; do not collect $200.

We tell you this only because you may not be aware of the danger involved in answering these questions incorrectly. And trust us, you will *always* answer them incorrectly. There is no right way to answer "Where do you want to eat?" when it is posed by your wife. Do not step into this minefield. If you nix Italian, she'll accuse you of thinking she's too fat to eat pasta. If you say no to Mexican, she'll think you're saying that she'll soon be wearing the cheese on her thighs. If you say that you really don't feel like a burger tonight, she'll think it has something to do with her hips. No matter what you say, your response will be reduced to one thing and one thing only—*that you think she's fat.* And heaven help you if you suggest a salad bar or anywhere that carries a diet plate. That's like signing a full "I think you're fat" confession.

Let's face it, we men are like goats. We can eat anything anywhere. So why should we complicate our lives by opening our mouths before there's any food in front of them? We should just agree to eat wherever our wives want to eat and not fight it. It's much safer that way.

What You Think It's About: Your driving.

What It's Really About: Your wife thinking, *I happen to know that you're not the brightest headlight on the grille. My mother knows it too. But since I can't say that to your face, I'm just going to tell you that you don't know how to drive.*

Let's be honest here: All vehicular arguing stems from something else and has nothing whatsoever to do with your driving. But your wife is going to make you *think* it's your driving to distract you from what is really going on in her head. Whether she says that you're going too fast, too slow, taking the longest route to get where you're going, not stopping to ask for directions—whatever it is—it doesn't matter. It all boils down to the simple fact that she believes she's smarter than you and wants to make sure you know it, too. But like we said, she doesn't want to just come right out and say that, because she loves you.

I (Rick) admit that my wife is smarter than me. I confess that to her all the time. Yet she'll still use the diversion of critiquing my driving instead of just coming right out and waving her report cards in my face. My wife and I have sometimes even driven separate cars to attend an event together, just so we'll both arrive in a relatively good mood. Sherri will constantly tell me how to drive, even after I've produced my driver's license to prove that I passed the test. But I just tell myself that it isn't about my driving, how many people I tailgated or cut off, or how many rolling stops I make. It's about deeper issues.

Even when I get lost, it's not about getting lost. It's about our SAT scores. And again, even though I admit she did better than me on the exam, some of our worst arguments have been over directional issues. My wife can be so convincing that she knows *exactly* where we're going—even though she's never been to the location and I've been there forty-three times—she can be so persuasive that I will yield to her because of the SAT score. But when we end up getting lost and it's clearly evident that I was right, will she apologize? Will she credit me back some points on the SAT or cut me some slack for a single C- on one of my report cards? Are you kidding me? She'll just look around and say, "Oh, wait a minute. This doesn't look right." Then she'll proceed to give me alternate instructions, which sound an awful lot like the direction I wanted to go in the first place.

What You Think It's About: Trying to decide what to do after pulling out of the church parking lot.

What It's Really About: Your wife is feeling such guilt over the Sunday morning sermon that she has to take it out on you in order to feel better about herself.

And while we're on the subject—has anyone but us noticed how so many pastors are afraid to take on moms on Mother's Day? We've never once heard a sermon on inattentive, uninvolved, or self-centered moms on Mother's Day. But let Father's Day roll around, and we dads get a tongue-lashing. Pastors wear us out on our day, while Mother's Day is more like All Saints' Day.

Think about it. When's the last time you heard dads being lifted up in a Father's Day service, instead of being given a list of what all they should be doing better? Moms get roses; we get the Ten Commandments of Fatherhood. Moms get chocolates; we dads get a moment of silence to reflect on how much time we spend at the office, hunting, fishing, or watching football.

And if you attend a church that has "testimony" time, then we're sure you've noticed this—wives testifying about their husbands' faults instead of their own. Can we have an amen?

"I just want to give praise that my husband, who I promised to love no matter what kind of an idiot he is, is finally starting to show some signs of intelligent life. Thank You, Lord!"

What's up with this, ladies? We're reasonably sure none of you would like it if your husband started sharing your shortcomings disguised as a testimony or prayer requests. Come on; let's admit it— prayer requests and testimonies can also be venting sessions. But don't worry; the pastor probably won't stop you. He won't take on a mother because he knows he has to come home and live with one himself.

What You Think It's About: Disciplining the children.

What It's Really About: Your wife is afraid that if you're not yelling or disciplining the kids as much as she is, your children are going to like you better.

At our (Rick's) house, it's like *Six Flags Over Dad*. The kids and I love to wrestle and mess around, and I'll admit, sometimes we have accidentally broken things. But we're having a good time. Still, Sherri will interrupt and tell us to "settle down." I don't understand this, because moments before the wrestling match, she was complaining that

I wasn't spending enough time with the kids. So which is it, ladies? Do you want us to help you with the kids or not? If you do, let us do it our way and have a little fun.

Do you want to know what I believe is really going on in most cases? Mom wants Dad to help, but only if he becomes an extension of her own style of parenting. As long as Dad follows Mom's rules and schedule, everything is fine. But should Dad deviate in any way from the "Mom standard" or should the kids appear to be having too much fun with Dad, then the amusement park must be closed down.

What You Think It's About: The temperature of the room.

What It's Really About: Reminding you once again that it is your wife's home. You might as well face it, husbands: you have little to no say in the day-to-day operations of your household. How many married men do I know who have picked out their living room drapes? None. How many have ever bought potpourri? None. Selected the coffee table? None. Lamps? None. Guys, we are living in our wives' homes. The sooner we realize this fact, the easier life will be for all of us. Accept this simple fact, and it'll be easy to surrender thermostat jurisdiction to your wife. (Besides, didn't we just tell you that we don't care anyway? See Rules of Engagement for Women, #4. That's our story, and we're stickin' to it!)

Unfortunately, the fact remains that many wives do not understand the concept of how air-conditioning and heating systems work. You don't walk into a room, feel a draft, and then slide the thermostat setting from 68 degrees all the way up to 88 degrees. Neither do you, when you start to feel a little bit warm, drop the thermostat down from 78 to iceberg. Adjustments on the thermostat should be ever so slight, and you shouldn't expect instantaneous warmth or coolness. It happens gradually. You have to give the unit time to do its job.

But again, guys, it's not our house.

What You Think It's About: Where to spend the holidays.

What It's Really About: Somehow your wife has detected that you'd rather go to your mom's house for Christmas, and she feels she has to trump you on this one. Even though your wife isn't all that crazy about her own family (you know this because of the numerous complaints she's made to you about them), she still doesn't want you to want to go to your mom's, especially on an occasion when your mother is going to be outdoing herself in the cooking department.

On a side note, husbands, never make the mistake of complimenting your mom's cooking in front of your wife. It's okay for your wife to compliment her cooking, but never let your wife hear *you* complimenting it. Always take your mother aside and do it privately.

What You Think It's About: What to watch at the movies.

What It's Really About: Keeping you from seeing a movie where the male lead is a strong character. We know in our own lives, our wives make us see every romantic comedy that comes along. Then, all the way home, they'll tell us how they wish we'd act more like the hero in the film. But when we do soften up and get all chick-flick-guy-star emotional, they talk about how weak we've become. To counter this, we suggest that you take your wife to see only action movies. The hero in action films is usually a jerk, and by comparison, we will always look better.

Lost Keys

Why is it when a woman loses her keys, it's always the husband's fault? Have you noticed this, guys? It doesn't matter who had the keys last; whether it was you or her, their disappearance will always be your fault.

"I can't find my keys. What'd you do with them?"

"What makes you think I did something with them?"

"Come on, quit playing around. Where are they?"

Sound familiar? Statistics say that every twelve minutes there is a wife somewhere in the world blaming her husband for losing her keys. (That's from our own personal survey among our friends, but we think we got the math right.)

Because this is such a widespread problem, we figured we should address it.

First of all, ladies, we are not the keepers of your keys, just as you are not the keepers of ours. If we lose our keys, do we accuse you? Okay, never mind, we'll move on.

All we're saying is: don't automatically assume that just because we had them last, we know where they are. We may have dropped them in your purse, in which case the responsibility falls back on you. We may have placed them on your side of the bed. Again, the responsibility would be yours at that point. Or we may have left them in the car.

Since it's your car, it would then be your responsibility. *See? There is no reason to unjustly accuse us of losing your keys.*

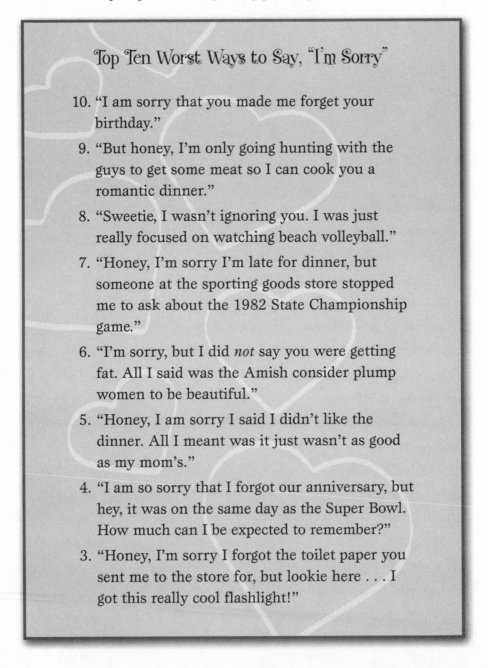

Top Ten Worst Ways to Say, "I'm Sorry"

10. "I am sorry that you made me forget your birthday."

9. "But honey, I'm only going hunting with the guys to get some meat so I can cook you a romantic dinner."

8. "Sweetie, I wasn't ignoring you. I was just really focused on watching beach volleyball."

7. "Honey, I'm sorry I'm late for dinner, but someone at the sporting goods store stopped me to ask about the 1982 State Championship game."

6. "I'm sorry, but I did *not* say you were getting fat. All I said was the Amish consider plump women to be beautiful."

5. "Honey, I am sorry I said I didn't like the dinner. All I meant was it just wasn't as good as my mom's."

4. "I am so sorry that I forgot our anniversary, but hey, it was on the same day as the Super Bowl. How much can I be expected to remember?"

3. "Honey, I'm sorry I forgot the toilet paper you sent me to the store for, but lookie here . . . I got this really cool flashlight!"

2. "Sweetheart, I am sorry I fell asleep during the movie you wanted us to watch together . . . but what does 'serendipity' mean, anyway?"

1. "I guess I'm sort of, well, you know, uh, I shouldn't have, uh, maybe I was acting like, well, you know, I didn't mean . . . aw, you know what I'm trying to say."

There is also the possibility, although remote, that we have hung the keys on the key hanger that you gave us last Christmas. This is unlikely since it has been medically proven that most men are missing the key hanger gene, but it is a possibility.

So the next time you're missing your keys, do us all a favor and just quietly look for them yourself. Retrace your steps, and then retrace the steps you think we might have taken. It will be so much easier if you leave us out of the whole situation. I think you'll agree that we're not that much of a help in the search anyway, so why take us away from the television set?

And one more thing: When you find your keys in the pocket of the jeans we were wearing yesterday—and you probably will—try not to gloat. That's so unbecoming, and it really bothers us. Besides, since it was you who bought those jeans for us last Christmas, along with the key hanger, the responsibility once again falls back to you. If you hadn't bought the jeans, the keys would not be in there. It's simple logic.

Now, where's the remote?

Betty's Payback

My (Bubba's) wife, Betty, has always done a great job of being a guest on our radio show. But there was one time when she made it a little more interesting than any of us expected.

One morning Betty called the station to give an on-the-air update about a desk that she had been shopping for. She expressed how she wanted a particular desk. I didn't really catch that part. But being a man and a problem solver, I just wanted to find a desk, buy it, and take it home. When I found a suitable desk, I showed it to her, and after some coaxing on my part, she said it would be fine.

This is where it was clearly Betty's duty to speak up if the desk wasn't "fine." Why is it that women fault us for believing what they tell us? If Betty says that the desk is fine, I'm going to believe that the desk is fine. Men connect the dots. What you say is what we believe. What you truly think doesn't come into the picture, because *we don't have a clue what you're thinking!*

So when Betty called the show to give an update on the desk and to say that she accidentally poured a cup of bleach on my new yellow DeWalt shirt, I was a little confused.

"What's wrong, honey?" I asked.

"I am going to the unfinished furniture store myself today," Betty told me—and our nationwide listening audience. "I want to get the desk I want, one that I can paint white and put gold knobs on."

Okay, sure, *now* she was being specific. She could have thrown in a few of those details last night at the store, I thought. But I didn't say that. Instead, I said, "Honey, I'm sorry for being insensitive to your needs and your wants in regards to your desk, and I'm sorry that I rushed you and made you pick out a desk you didn't really want."

And I meant it. Men, you know how we are—we run into a store and it's like a race. We grab the first thing that looks like the item we want, and we take it directly to the checkout counter. It doesn't matter if we got a deal or if it's even the correct item. The important thing is how quickly we made it in and out of the store. *Four minutes, thirty seconds! A new record!*

So I wasn't about to fight it. I'm a man and know my ways. So I admitted my fault in that. Still, Betty should have spoken up. And I told her so. "Betty, why didn't you just say, 'No, Bill, I don't want that one. I want a white one with gold knobs'?"

"Well, I did—sort of," Betty said, trying to defend herself. "I kept saying I would like to have a lighter one. I didn't hit you over the head with a sledgehammer or anything like that, but I thought I had gotten the point across."

This is where you might really need legal counsel.

"Mrs. Bussey, did you or did you not tell Mr. Bussey, 'I want a white desk with gold knobs. I do not want the one you're looking at'?"

"Well, I, uh—"

"Just answer the question, Mrs. Bussey."

"I guess maybe I didn't—"

"You didn't what, Mrs. Bussey?"

"I didn't specifically tell Mr. Bussey that I wanted a white desk with gold knobs."

"You didn't *specifically say that you wanted a white desk with gold knobs, and yet, and yet, Mrs. Bussey, you expected him to know that you wanted a white desk with gold knobs. Is that correct?"*

"Yes."

"No further questions."

See, it's all about communication, ladies. Don't assume that we know what you want us to know if you're not telling us what you want us to know; know what we mean?

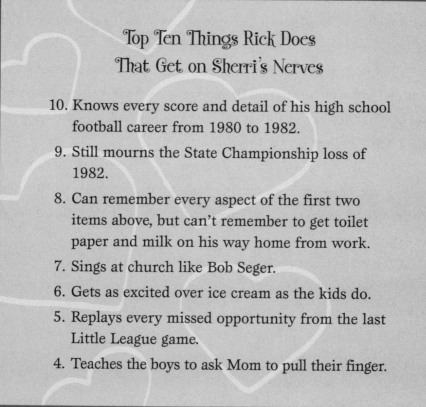

Top Ten Things Rick Does That Get on Sherri's Nerves

10. Knows every score and detail of his high school football career from 1980 to 1982.

9. Still mourns the State Championship loss of 1982.

8. Can remember every aspect of the first two items above, but can't remember to get toilet paper and milk on his way home from work.

7. Sings at church like Bob Seger.

6. Gets as excited over ice cream as the kids do.

5. Replays every missed opportunity from the last Little League game.

4. Teaches the boys to ask Mom to pull their finger.

3. Puts dishes in the dishwasher without rinsing them first. (Rick: "Hey, I thought it was a dish*washer*!")

2. Asks for ketchup at five-star restaurants.

1. Thinks referees can hear him at his son's high school football games and that they welcome his input and advice.

Top Sixteen Things That Bubba Does That Get on Betty's Nerves

(We've been married longer, so Betty has a longer list!)

16. At least once a month, bases our family Bible study on the Song of Solomon.

15. Constantly debates the long-term attributes of HGTV vs. the NASA Channel.

14. Constantly uses the "B" word: *Budget!*

13. Totally lacks appreciation for the importance of window dressing.

12. Maintains tight rotation of his four favorite pairs of underwear, along with readiness to explain why the rest of the pairs in the drawer don't measure up. (Bubba: "And while we're on this subject, why is it that they're called a

pair of underwear when it's only *one*? Can anybody answer that?")

11. Repeatedly demonstrates inability to buy a pair of jeans alone and to find a pair that was designed and sold after 2001.

10. Expresses "only child" complex—doesn't want anyone touching his stuff, to the point that he keeps his stuff locked up from the rest of the family. This is a little paranoid on his part. (Bubba: "I think it means I've still got all my stuff.")

9. Forgets something and needs me to bring it to him, but I can't get to it because everything is locked up (refer to Bubba Annoyance #10).

8. Justifies thousands and thousands of dollars in outdoor, hunting, and high-tech electronics, but argues that the $265 spent at Wal-Mart was a budget buster!

7. Requests that I do my part to help him lose weight by cooking low-fat meals—*after* stuffing himself on casseroles, pies, cookies, and anything with cheese for four hours at the studio.

6. Demonstrates complete cluelessness regarding the proper way to hang pictures, evidenced by hanging them so high that only a seven-foot man could see them.

5. Has an uncontrollable desire to show up thirty minutes early everywhere.

4. Can sit patiently in the woods all day and not see a single thing and still want to go back the next morning, but can't go shopping and wait two minutes for me to try on a dress.

3. Constantly asks me to go hunting with him, but will never volunteer to go to Christmas Village with me.

2. Gets the same stomach virus that ravaged the entire family, but requires an ER visit, IV fluids, and rehab—while the rest of us just nobly fought our way through it *on our own*.

1. Causes me to have to read about myself in *New York Times* best-selling books. (Bubba: "She complains about it, but she'll still cash the check.")

Things Betty Does That Get on Bubba's Nerves

1. Has the nerve to come up with her list a lot quicker than I can come up with mine.

Blind Spots

Show us a good marriage, and we'll show you a union of two good forgivers. In fact, one reason the divorce rate is so high, especially among Christians, is that many of us have forgotten how to forgive. And one reason for that is we have a blind spot to our own need for forgiveness.

When Jesus taught us to pray, "Forgive us our debts as we forgive our debtors," He was demonstrating how God reserves the right to tie our own forgiveness to how completely we forgive others. Grace is a free gift, but if we withhold it from those around us, He might withhold it from us.

Remember the story in the Bible about the unmerciful servant? This man owed the king a huge amount of money, but when he couldn't pay his debt, he begged the king for mercy. The king took pity on him and forgave the entire debt. Then this same man ran into another man who owed him a mere pittance; basically, it was pennies compared to millions. Instead of being merciful, as the king had been merciful to him, the man demanded that his debtor pay up. When the debtor couldn't, in an act of extreme moral arrogance, the unmerciful servant had his debtor thrown into jail.

When the king heard about this, he was pretty ticked off. He reinstated the unmerciful servant's original debt and threw *him* into prison!

In our marriages, God wants us to be good forgivers, knowing full well that we ourselves have been forgiven. The Bible tells us that we have all sinned, and since all sin is looked upon equally by God, there is no room for self-righteousness.

But most of us try to make room for it anyway, don't we? We want our own faults or failures overlooked or forgiven, but then we want the book thrown at the next guy or, more often than not, at our spouse. That's not how God intended marriage to be.

Besides two good forgivers, a good marriage also requires two good scorekeepers.

It's like sports. If the scorekeeper kept only his favorite team's score, it wouldn't be much of a game, would it?

"So what's the score?"

"Ten."

"Ten to what?"

"I don't know—just ten."

"Who's got ten?"

"We do."

"What's the other team's score?"

"I dunno. I was just keeping score for our team."

That sounds crazy, but it's what we sometimes do in our marriages. When we wrap our minds around the concept of keeping a more accurate scorecard, however, along with the fact that we need forgiveness every day, we become humble, and that turns us into good forgivers.

How many marriages could be saved if we would just be a little more thorough when seeing our own faults, and a lot less judgmental when seeing our mate's?

"You Gonna Eat That?"

I (Bubba) don't understand my wife—or maybe all women, for that matter. Why is it that women pick the worst possible time to talk to us about losing weight—usually when we're just about to take a bite?

Betty does this all the time. She'll talk to me about my need to diet, as she's scooping another helping of mashed potatoes onto my plate.

"Here, would you like another helping of this?" she'll say temptingly and then add, "Bill, when are you going to lose some weight? Seriously, you really need to think about it. . . . Is this enough, or do you want another biscuit, too?"

Come on, ladies, admit you do this. You keep us husbands on such a yo-yo, it's no wonder so many of us end up looking like one.

If you really want us to shed a few pounds, why don't you talk about it when we're at the gym? Stand by the exercise bike and tell us how great we're starting to look in our T-shirt. Don't do it when you've just handed us a warm and gooey cinnamon roll that you brought home from the mall. What are we supposed to do? Refuse the sweet and insult you? We're far too sensitive to do that. Why, we'd eat the whole pan of cinnamon rolls if it would make you feel better about yourself. We'd gladly make that kind of sacrifice for the woman we love.

The bottom line is this, ladies: If you want us to be the same size we were at our wedding, you've got to help us. Quit with the temptations!

Don't park the Oreos on our side of the coffee table. In fact, don't leave an open package of Oreos anywhere in the house. That's what the safety deposit box at the bank is for.

You can't have it both ways. You can't expect us to look like the *Bachelor* when you're feeding us like we're Doug from *King of Queens*. It just doesn't work like that. Too many calories equal weight gain. Simple as that.

But since this behavior of yours seems to be a problem for many husbands, we thought it would be helpful if we offered the following guide to wives everywhere:

What You'd Like for Us to Do	What You Can Do to Help
Lose weight.	Stop deep-frying the Twinkies.
Be nicer to your friends, family, boss, and coworkers.	Quit venting to us about them. (Our natural instinct is to be your protector.)
Drive more slowly.	Stop talking about how late we're going to be and why it's going to be our fault.
Make more money.	Don't complain when we go to work.
Talk to you more.	Stop keeping us from getting a word in edgewise.

Help out more with the kids.	Don't criticize us for not playing/feeding/dressing/burping/changing/doing homework or anything else the exact same way you do. Moms and dads have different styles of child rearing. It gives our children a good balance. Accept that.
Be sensitive to your interests.	Don't be insensitive to ours. "Guy stuff" may not be interesting to you, but it is to us.
Be more romantic.	Don't compare us to your friends' husbands. That does nothing for our self-esteem.
Do more chores around the house.	Stop critiquing them after we're done.
Watch less football on TV.	Stand in front of the television set looking beautiful, if you know what we mean. But we'd better have TiVo!

Teamwork

Rick: A lot of men do it, and they do it successfully. We, however, are pretty sure it wouldn't work for us. What are we talking about? Working with our spouses.

We can see it now: We'd be on the radio, trying to set up one of our comedy segments or talking to a listener or celebrity guest, and our wives would be in the background, asking us why we didn't take the trash out or help with the dishes before we left the house that morning.

"That's all fun and entertaining, Rick," Sherri would say. "But are you going to give me any help around the house? Can you just put the dishes in the sink, Rick? *Can't you just get them to the sink, and then you can get back to your listeners?*"

At least she doesn't ask me to load the dishwasher. Not anymore, anyway. I hate loading the dishes, and I have a foolproof plan to keep us guys as far away from that appliance as possible. Simply follow my instructions, men, and you will never again have to load the dishwasher. I did it myself with Sherri, and it worked like a charm. I was going insane loading and unloading the dishwasher every night, so I just started putting stuff away in the most bizarre places, places where I knew Sherri would have a hard time finding them.

"Hey, Rick, have you seen my spatula? I've been looking every . . . wait a minute; what's it doing here in this flowerpot?"

"Rick, have you seen the skillet? . . . Is that it over there on the bookcase, behind the DVDs?"

To speed up your release from kitchen duty, I also suggest leaving a plastic cup near the heating element of the dishwasher. Do that one time, let it smoke up the kitchen real good, and before you know it, you're a free man!

If neither of the above works, I have other tricks worth trying. For instance, put an unbreakable glass, not on the upper rack where it belongs, but down where the bottom spinner is. This drives them crazy, especially when they hear it being bounced around during the wash cycle.

Or let a cooking utensil dangle down from the upper rack so that the middle spinner bangs against it every time it goes around. You may have to really work to wedge it down in there, but the *ping-ping*ing of the spinner against it will be enough to cut your kitchen duty sentence in half. And if they can't pull out the top drawer because the utensil is caught on something in the bottom drawer, you might be granted instant freedom.

I should note that it's important to have your facial expressions match the severity of the infraction. Look contrite. Whatever you do, don't laugh. *Naive* is the operative word. For this to work, you have to appear innocent; you must present yourself as having the best of intentions. Can you help it if that wooden spoon wanted to wrap itself around the strainer handle like that?

When Sherri finally gave up and told me, "Please, don't ever load the dishwasher again," I kept the celebration internal. On the outside, I looked like she had crushed my feelings, and even went so far as to say, "Well, if that's the way you're going to be about it. What's next? You're going to tell me to go ahead and leave my underwear on the floor because I don't pick them up right, either? Is that where this relationship is going? Is that what you want me to do? Not ever pick up my clothes again, leave you all the dishes to do, and not make my half of the bed? Is that what [*I choked up here*] you want me to say? I'm human, too, Sherri. I've got feelings. I want to feel like I'm contributing to the running of the household in some way. But if you want to take that away from me, that's okay. I'll just go downstairs and be alone. Don't try to make me change my mind on this. You can't possibly understand how this rejection makes me feel."

This is what is known as *reverse psychology*. It's taking the weapons that our wives, since the beginning of marriage, have used against us and then turning the tables on them.

But eventually most wives will catch on. I got away with it for quite a while, but then Sherri started giving me that look that says, "I know what you're doing, Rick. I know you melted that plastic bowl on purpose, and I also know you purposely washed the darks with the lights in the washing machine just so you wouldn't have to do laundry anymore. Don't think for one minute that you're fooling me. And I hope you enjoy wearing your new pink underwear."

Until they do catch on, though, it'll buy you a lot of free passes from kitchen duty.

Bubba: I have tried Rick's method, but it wasn't so easy to pull it off on Betty. She found it hard to believe that I could configure an entire computer system, get on the Internet, visit any site in the world, and pull down valuable information, but could not figure out how to set the washing machine. She wouldn't buy into the fact that I get confused over the whole cold/warm/hot thing. But come on, ladies, admit it. It *is* confusing. How are we supposed to know which clothes get which temperature? There wasn't a class for this in our schools.

The way I see it, the washing machine dial is like kryptonite. If you get anywhere around it, it will weaken you, just like it did Superman.

But my wife and I agree that doing the laundry is not all that exciting. She doesn't want to do it any more than I do. I'm just better at finding a way to get out of household chores than she is. Like Rick says, it's all a matter of falling even shorter than their expectations and then you're a free man.

Personally, I've been banned from washing clothes, washing dishes, dusting, cleaning the windows, and basically, doing anything around the house that involves a cleanser, a squeegee, or feathers on a stick. Betty says it's easier for her to do it herself than it is to go behind me and fix what I've messed up.

So, yes, for the record, Rick's plan does work like a charm. But then there is a price to pay for all this freedom. It means that the household maintenance schedule is totally up to our wives. It means that if they choose to vacuum during the Super Bowl or run a load of wash during the World Series, we really have no leg to stand on. And it also means that they get to move our things wherever they want to in order to dust.

It is that last issue, the moving of our stuff, that gives us pause. We husbands like our things in their place. We enjoy hunting when we're outdoors, but we don't want to hunt for anything in our homes.

Some days it's like being in the middle of a scavenger hunt. We'll hand our wives a list of our things that they have misplaced that week, and we'll see which one of us can find all the items first. They usually just laugh, though, shove the list in their purse, and then go shopping.

This is, of course, a completely different response than what we give them when they ask us to help them look for something.

Rick: Whenever Sherri needs me to help her find an item she's misplaced, I will immediately sweep the room with one glance. Sure, I could open a few cupboards and drawers and look inside them, but it's not in my nature.

"Sorry, babe," I'll say, winded from the glance. "It's not here. I don't know where it's at."

"Could you move a box, Rick, *just one box,* and look for it?"

Again, that's not in the male nature. Men don't want to move something to look behind it for anything. We know scary things hide behind boxes (it's from our childhood and one too many Stephen King movies). So if the item isn't in plain view, to us it's lost.

We will, however, climb through waist-high brush in utter blackness and then climb into a cobweb- and possibly snake-infested hunting house to spend the morning waiting on a buck that never shows up. But don't ask us to move a box of books with visible dust bunnies. Some of those bunnies could be rabid!

And while we're on the subject of misplaced items, why is it that no one in the house ever knows where the scissors are? My dream is to have one place for the scissors and for them to be in that same place every day. Is that too much to ask? I realize it wasn't in our marriage vows (when we renew them, this will be number one), but it is aggravating.

One day not long ago, I finally took it upon myself to solve the dilemma. I bought nine pairs of scissors and placed them strategically around the house. I had a pair everywhere you could imagine. Whenever Sherri would ask if I knew where the scissors were, I'd simply go to one of my secret hiding places and say, "Yeah, I've got them right here." Then when she'd ask another time, I'd just go to one of the other secret places and there they would be. Sherri thought I was somehow finding the same pair.

Helpmates—that's all Bubba and I want to be to our wives . . .

So remember: whether you're hiding scissors, loading the dishwasher, or setting the *correct* laundry temperature, the bottom line is, marriage goes a lot smoother when both parties help with the chores.

Top Ten Reasons Wives Nag

10. They've watched too many television shows for preschoolers and believe that constant repetition is the key to learning.
9. Some women simply can't get the concept of "Don't think out loud."
8. Nagging is one of the few love languages a husband understands.
7. They've given up on asking their husbands to cuddle.
6. They know that braying animal sound will get the husband's attention.

5. It cuts through every attempt by the husband to listen selectively.

4. Without those complaints, the husband would not know the difference between being home and being out with the guys.

3. They can't nag their girlfriends because friends wouldn't stand for it. And door-to-door salesmen have the freedom to move on to the next house. So who's left? The husband.

2. It's a test to see whether the husband will put up with it or whether he loves only the "perfect" her.

1. Nagging is one of only two ways guaranteed to get the husband to eventually see things her way.

Last-Minute Shopping

Husbands, let's be honest. How many times have you found your-self in the grocery store, drugstore, or mall on the night before your anniversary, on Valentine's Day, or on Christmas Eve, patheti-cally trying to find a card or gift for the woman you love?

I'm sure the whole world would agree that it is a sad sight to see all the procrastinating husbands lined along aisle six of the grocery store on Valentine's Day at 5:48 in the evening, arm wrestling each other for the last six cards left on the rack or playing tug-of-war over that last bouquet of fresh-cut flowers.

Why do we do it? Why do we procrastinate when it comes to show-ing the woman we love how much we love her? Is it because we're having such a hard time expressing the depth of our love that we end up taking longer than we should to select our gifts or even bypassing them altogether?

Nice try.

There really is no excuse. Even if we have no money, we can still make her a card or gift out of our office supplies or whatever's in the garage.

The Rick and Bubba solution to perpetual special occasion amnesia is to plan ahead.

Husbands, let's be honest. You *know* you have an anniversary coming every year. The date does not sneak up on you. So write it down in your date book, and look at it from time to time. You might also want to watch for hints that your wife may be giving you, hints such as carving "Happy Anniversary" in your bath soap or drawing hearts in ketchup on your slice of meat loaf.

Once you're aware of the date, the next step is to do something about it—before the last minute. Start shopping for your gift and card at least a week in advance. That way you can be more selective.

In the card department, may we make a suggestion? Wives love sentimental cards. And they like to laugh. We say go ahead and get that funny card, but buy a serious one, too. Share your heart in the serious one. Wives love that.

When it comes to gifts, hopefully you've been paying close attention to any hints your wife has been dropping over the previous few months. Most wives will let you know exactly what they'd like for their anniversary, but you need to listen. In fact, for some women, that's the gift they want—*for their husbands to listen!*

But since it's hard to wrap that up in a gift, listen to their conversation and try to pick up on any hints that they're giving you for more tangible gifts. If you're still stumped, then remember this one simple, fast rule of gift-giving: Give your wife something *she* wants, not something you'd like for her to have. Product return lines would be so much shorter the day after Christmas if we would only remember that one simple rule. Few people actually write "reindeer slippers" on their wish list.

As far as where to go on your anniversary, if you don't have a lot of money, you don't have to go anywhere. You can easily prepare a romantic candlelight dinner at home for just the two of you. Send the kids over to Grandma and Grandpa's house; take off the ripped T-shirt and put on your Sunday best instead. Play some romantic music on the radio or CD player, build a fire in the fireplace, and celebrate your wife. If you don't have a fireplace, turn up the heater until it feels like you're sitting in front of a roaring fire.

Your anniversary comes only once a year, so don't miss this opportunity to rekindle the romance and remind yourselves how much you mean to each other.

But try not to get so sidetracked that you burn the steaks.

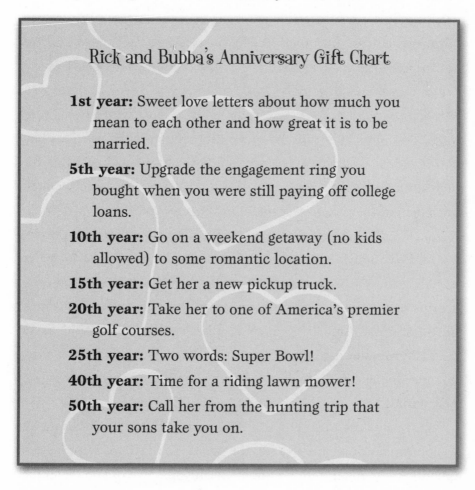

Rick and Bubba's Anniversary Gift Chart

1st year: Sweet love letters about how much you mean to each other and how great it is to be married.

5th year: Upgrade the engagement ring you bought when you were still paying off college loans.

10th year: Go on a weekend getaway (no kids allowed) to some romantic location.

15th year: Get her a new pickup truck.

20th year: Take her to one of America's premier golf courses.

25th year: Two words: Super Bowl!

40th year: Time for a riding lawn mower!

50th year: Call her from the hunting trip that your sons take you on.

Showers of Popcorn

In the lives of every married couple, there will be moments of hilarity, often known only to the two of them. These private jokes, sometimes called "inside humor," often make for some of the biggest belly laughs a husband and wife will share in their entire lives together.

Betty and I (Bubba) collected another such moment not long ago while at our local movie theater. Even though it's our own private joke, we are sharing it here in the privacy of these pages. (Besides, since there were witnesses involved, it's not all that private anyway.)

When we first arrived at the movie theater, we did what we usually do—we headed straight for the snack bar. We ordered a couple of giant sodas and the biggest tub of popcorn available—you know, the size that you can bathe the kids in later. We also ordered the supersize box of Whoppers, and an assortment of other stuff, all of which ran our total up to approximately one and a half times our house payment. In no other place would we pay these kinds of prices, but for some reason, at a movie theater, we do.

Laden with all our goodies, it was now time to get to our theater of choice and find a good seat. Since we had taken a little longer than expected at the snack bar, the previews were already in progress by the time we entered. This theater also had steep, elevated seating, much like stadium seating. This made our navigation in the dark that much more difficult, especially with the buffet of junk food that we were carrying. But eventually we did spot a couple of empty seats.

As we climbed over the knees of the people already seated in our aisle, we were excitedly grabbing handfuls of our popcorn like a couple of eight-year-olds. We both love popcorn, and movie popcorn is the best. With a ladle or two of hot butter drizzled all over it, nothing could be better. We were getting butter all over our hands and faces, and we didn't care. You're supposed to get a little slimy eating movie popcorn, right?

What followed, however, was definitely not in our plans.

As we neared our seats, Betty, whose hands were, like I said, quite greasy, somehow lost hold of the giant bucket of popcorn and ended up dumping the better half of it on top of the couple seated directly in front of us. It was like something out of a slapstick comedy: they each had a target drawn on their scalps, and Betty hit the bull's-eye. Thankfully, all this couple could see when they looked up was hot buttered popcorn raining down and two shadowy figures in the dark.

I tried apologizing, on behalf of my wife, to both shadowy figures, but they didn't say a word. I was afraid the woman was going to slap me because she had taken so much of the butter to her hair, so I sat down quickly and tried to push back as far as I could in my seat to get out of her reach.

Betty attempted to dust them off, but it was like a snow bank. The more we brushed to the side, the more piled up. And most of it wouldn't let go of their clothes. Those kernels were sticking to them like packing peanuts to fingers.

Once we realized the other couple wasn't going to physically punch us over the incident, we began to relax and enjoy the movie. We may have relaxed a little too much, though, because we started getting tickled over the whole situation. We tried not to laugh out loud, but it wasn't easy. It was like when someone has an intestinal problem in church, and you know that if you laugh at his bodily noises, you're going to make him mad. So you try your best to hold it in (which *he* should have done, too). But you can't hold in your laughter because you know what just happened really *was* funny. Especially if it happened during the song service and sounded like blasts from the tuba section at the perfect musical moment.

But back to the popcorn. Betty was at least covering her mouth and being more discreet with her laughter than I was. I lost it every time I looked at their fluffy hairdos, which now looked like someone had poured a full bottle of yellow mousse down on them. You could have fried half a chicken in all the butter that was slowly dripping down their necks and foreheads.

This couple was going to have to spend hours in the shower that night, just trying to degrease themselves—and that wasn't even counting the time it was going to take to pick all the popcorn out of the drain. It's no wonder then that after the movie, Betty and I chose to remain in our seats and let them leave first. When they rose to their feet, I noticed there were still pieces of popcorn stuck to the woman's back, and for a brief moment, I thought about brushing them off, but quickly decided against it.

To this day I don't know who that couple was. But I have to say, we owe them. They have provided a private story and more belly laughs for Betty and me since that unfortunate incident than you could imagine. We think about them every time we walk into a dark theater with a bucket of popcorn. And I have a feeling they've spent a good amount of time thinking of us, too.

Lookin' Good

Being MOWs (Men of Weight), we have had to step it up a bit in the "coolness" department. Let's face it: Few girls grow up hoping their real-life Ken doll will also have a gut. So for us to be appealing to our wives (or back then, our girlfriends), we have had to find ways to cover our weight and still look hip. Not that weight is a negative. It isn't. We're big and proud of it. Still, it doesn't hurt to have a little cool thrown in the mix, too.

One style that seems to work for us is camouflage. You do have to be a little careful with the pattern, though. Your goal is to look like a tall, lean tree, not a short, squat bush. Both are possible with camouflage, so if you plan to try this technique, check the pattern closely to make sure it's the look you're going for.

If you're trying to come off as cool, you might also want to reduce the amount of hunter's orange that you wear. Despite what many men think, it's not the dream of most women to look up and see a navel orange with legs winking at them. Come on, guys, use your heads. There's a reason you've never seen the Kool-Aid pitcher guy on the cover of *People* magazine. He's got a good smile, but how many dates is he getting? Exactly. Again, weight isn't the issue. It's the colors we wear and how we carry ourselves.

Besides camouflage, we've also tried the popular "fin down the middle of our hair" look. You know, that short Mohawk that a lot of guys are wearing right now. Both Bubba and I have large heads, so our fins don't stand up very tall, and we usually end up looking like someone took a marker to our scalps.

I (Rick) have to confess that I fell into the mullet craze when it was popular. I thought it would make me look cool. Oh, how wrong I was. Now when I look at old photos of myself, *cool* is not the word that comes to mind. All you former mullet-wearers out there, *what were we thinking?* Was our desire to impress women so strong that we sacrificed our own dignity?

This behavior didn't just start with the mullet, though. We've been doing this sort of thing to ourselves throughout all of history. Do you really think George Washington wanted to wear those short pants, high heels, and a powdered wig? No way! He was just trying to impress Martha. Do you think Napoleon liked his hair cut like that? Are you kidding me? It had to have been Josephine's idea.

What about the Victorian era? What were we thinking with those puffy sleeves? No wonder by the time the Wild West rolled around, we went overboard on the testosterone. We wore jackets made from the hides of animals we'd shot and started growing as much facial hair as we could. Would we have done any of that if it weren't for our puffy-sleeve phase?

So yes, the mullet was a mistake. I admit that. But I have since learned to be more selective with the fashion trends that come along. I don't have to jump on the bandwagon and change my look just because some Hollywood celebrity or New York fashion model does it. I can wear camo and always look cool . . . as long as the mullet photo never surfaces.

Betty's Top Ten Reasons Why Bubba Has a Hard Time Losing Weight

10. He's reduced his caloric intake by one-third, but it's still *twice* the recommended daily allowance.

9. He thinks the idea of a shake for breakfast, a shake for lunch, and a sensible dinner is two large chocolate shakes from Dairy Queen and an all-you-can-eat buffet.

8. He's on a one-man mission to consume enough red meat to prove mad cow disease was all a hoax.

7. He found out where the beef was twenty years ago, and we haven't been able to keep him away since.

6. He keeps confusing the bathroom scales with some antigravity scales from NASA.

5. His idea of pumping iron is swinging a golf club every now and then, and riding in a golf cart with snacks and a beverage service.

4. He's sure that he read somewhere that "one sleeve of a box of Girl Scout cookies equals one serving."

3. When Bubba saw the "Eat Mor Chikin" slogan from Chick-fil-A, he thought it just said "Eat Mor."

2. For Bubba, jogging is not a good enough reason to get hot and sweaty.

1. It's too hard to calculate your caloric intake when you've got a chicken leg in one hand and a brownie in the other.

Bubba Unplugged

Like some husbands, if I (Bubba) have something that I'm excited about, I plunge right into it. With me, there's no holding back. I've got to have it all. I wouldn't say I have an addictive personality, but like the Bible says, "That which I do, I do with all my heart" (or something like that . . .). If I'm going to do it, I'm going to give it my 100 percent.

Such is the case with tennis.

Before I go on, I should tell you that it was Betty who first got me into the sport. I noticed something interesting happened each time she left the house to go play a round of tennis—she'd leave me behind! Not just behind, but behind with a list of chores to do! And she'd leave the kids behind, too, for me to babysit! That's when I decided that perhaps I, too, should grab a racket and check out this game of tennis. So yes, I confess: I became a tennis player simply from desperation to get out of the house and to get out of doing chores.

Even with my less-than-perfect motives, I still took tennis seriously. I had to have all the latest gear. I had to have the right tennis clothes, the right tennis racket, and the right tennis balls. I lived and breathed tennis. (Well, the first few games I just lived and *wheezed* tennis.)

But tennis turned out to be a healthy sport for me. I ended up dropping about twenty pounds, all thanks to the workout I would get every time we played. Don't get me wrong—there's still plenty of me left. I'm not going to blow away in an Alabama wind gust or anything like that. But people have noticed my weight loss enough to ask if Rick and I are still going to be able to stay with our "sexiest fat men alive" slogan. I tell them, "Well, the last time I strolled past a mirror, the slogan was safe."

This passion I have for new adventures has a downside, though. I get so zoned into something that I have a hard time letting go of it, long after I should. Like when we're cutting up on the radio show or at the office, I get so caught up in the sarcasm that I make the mistake of bringing that attitude home with me. I want to verbally spar with Betty, like I'd been doing with Rick all morning. I'll end up saying something that would have been hysterical had I said it to Rick, but when I say it to my wife, it just doesn't come off the same. Even as the words are tumbling out of my mouth, I'm wanting to pull them back. I'm thinking, *What am I doing?* at the very moment I'm doing it. But it's too late.

That happened again not long ago—on the tennis court. Monday is our family tennis lesson day. I'm usually the first to take a thirty-minute drill; then the kids take theirs, and then all of us together do some drills.

On this particular Monday, I'd come straight from the studio and had been working out with the kids before Betty even got there. And if I do say so myself, I was doing great—running, hustling, and making all my moves perfectly.

But then Betty walked up. I don't know if she did this on purpose, but she happened to arrive just as I was trying on some new sunglasses. I don't know what the fancy-schmancy brand name was, but they have a green lens and are designed especially for tennis players. When you look through these special lenses, everything appears kind of a bleak, green color. Everything, that is, except for the tennis ball.

It is fluorescent yellow and really stands out. That's what makes them such good glasses for tennis players.

Now the simple fact that I would buy tennis glasses so I could see the tennis ball better is classic Bubba. But I figured since I needed a new pair of sunglasses anyway, why not buy some that would improve my game? The fact that I could never wear these glasses while driving because I wouldn't be able to see what color the traffic lights were didn't deter me. I had to have them. I also thought I looked rather good in them.

Betty had a different opinion.

"I hope you're not going to get those glasses," she said when she walked up to me.

"Why?" I asked.

"They make you look like a bug." Actually, I thought that sounded like a pretty good look for me. But she continued, "They're hideous, Bill. Take them off."

I thought "hideous" was a little strong, so still being in studio mode, I shot back, "Well, that's pretty funny coming from someone who looks like they've been eating ice cream."

Now, I knew she hadn't been eating ice cream. My comment was in reference to a dry skin problem that she had on her face at the time (that may or may not have resembled smeared ice cream). And it would have been really funny had I said that to Rick. But it probably wasn't the best comeback for my lovely wife, Betty Lou. I should have been more sensitive to her eczema outbreak, just as she should have been more sensitive to my buggy glasses. But in marriage we don't always use wisdom.

Betty's hand shot up onto her hip, and I had to jump back as quickly as I could to get out of tennis racket reach—not that she would ever have swung her racket at me. It was simply a preemptive measure.

Betty proceeded to let me know how insensitive my comment was. (Rick never would have complained.) But it was an important lesson learned: Know your audience. That's basic Comedy 101 stuff. I should have known better.

If a woman has any little thing wrong with her—a pimple, dry skin, whatever—she is probably hypersensitive about it. It would be smart to leave the subject alone. But I wasn't using the good parts of my brain that day. When my beloved got on me about the glasses, I went into my "I must defend myself and say the first thing that comes to mind" mode.

Needless to say, the ride home wasn't much fun. And the incident was even less funny that night in bed.

Note to self (and anyone who wants to gain wisdom from my mistakes): If your wife is hurt, embarrassed, or upset over a "funny" remark you made, you're probably not doing comedy.

Top Ten Reasons Some Husbands Don't Pick Up After Themselves

10. They're making sure they can find their stuff again.
9. Because then they might have to actually put it away or wash it.
8. It's a bread trail back to the bathroom.
7. It takes them back to their college days.
6. They're still waiting on Mom to do it.
5. They're leaving behind emergency underwear.

4. They love their wives too much to make them feel unneeded.

3. They're too busy working tirelessly to do their part to provide for their families—and watching TV.

2. They're rushing to the kids' rooms to get one of them to pull their finger.

1. If they stopped, what would comedians have to joke about?

His Money—Her Money—
One Big Headache

As financial guru and our good friend Dave Ramsey might say—*for better, for worse* carries over into your balance sheet, too. In a marriage there shouldn't be any "his money–her money" attitudes going on. No matter who the major breadwinner is, the money belongs to both of you. So do the bills. Financial decisions should be a team effort.

Some couples today, however, operate under the assumption that the man's check pays the bills and the woman's check is her own money, to do with as she pleases. This is how the budget plan looks in those marriages:

His Money	Her Money
Mortgage	Personal savings account (in case marriage doesn't work out)
Car payments, insurance, and repairs	One car wash every third Thursday

Wife's beauty salon treatment	Tip for stylist, but only if not already included in credit card transaction
Heating for house	New jacket
$300 phone bill	Luncheon with girlfriends
Household groceries	Figure-enhancing surgery
Dining out	Gum
Family vacation	Electrolysis
Both his and her credit card payments	The stamps for mailing them
Life insurance	Increased premium for additional coverage

Are you sensing a pattern here, guys? There's a reason marriage is supposed to be a partnership in all things: to make sure you remain a team. Before we get too smug, we should point out that it's not just women who do this sort of manipulating. It could just as easily be the other way around—with the wife's money paying all the bills and the husband's money spent on frivolous things.

It doesn't really matter which one of you is benefiting from this sort of arrangement; neither does it matter how much or how little extra money we're talking about. What matters is the answer to this question: *Are you being fair to your mate and your marriage when it comes to money issues?*

When you said, "I do," that meant you would work together as a team in every aspect of your marriage—the upkeep of your home, your relationship, your parenting, and your finances. When both sides are putting into the kitty and both sides are deciding how that kitty is going to be spent, you all end up ahead in the financial department. Two heads are better than one. And so are two wallets, working together, no matter how empty or how full.

"We're" Pregnant?

It didn't used to be this way, but these days, husbands are expected to participate more in the pregnancy process—beyond our initial participation, that is. It's even gotten to the point where husbands are saying things like, *"We're* pregnant" or *"We've* got an appointment at the OB-GYN's office."

Does that sound natural to you? It's not that we're against having children; we're certainly not. In fact, we've gotten pretty good at *"pro-creating"* over the years. But the times (and our wives) continue to demand more and more male participation in the matter, so much so that I (Rick) feel the need to warn other husbands about what awaits them on that first visit to an OB-GYN's office.

First of all, you're going to feel uncomfortable from the time you step through the door. It is not you, so forget checking for mismatched shoes or smelling your armpits. It is simply the situation. You are a foreigner in their land. You are welcome, but you don't speak their language or understand their customs, and since you aren't showing the physical signs of a pregnancy, such as a protruding stomach and stretch marks, you are considered an alien. (Bubba and I do have the protruding stomach, but no stretch marks yet, so I don't think that counts.)

I suggest bringing your own reading material for the time you'll spend in the waiting room. There will be magazines, but all of them will be about pregnancy, nursing, and maternity fashions. You won't find a single copy of *Guns & Ammo* or *Field & Stream*.

You might be tempted to bring a PSP with you to the doctor visit, or some other electronic device to play with while you wait, but I don't recommend it. All the pregnant women in the room will look at you like you're some sort of insensitive jerk who is not stepping up to the plate to support his wife.

Once the nurse calls your family name and they take you back into the examination room, things get even more uncomfortable. There are so many strange things in there, you won't know where to look. You'll see equipment that'll make your whole body squirm. Ladies, you know what I'm talking about. I grew up watching westerns, so the term *stir-rups* is nothing new to me. But Clint Eastwood and John Wayne never had to shove their boots into a pair of them at *that* angle. Just looking at those things makes my head hurt.

Again, you're in a foreign land. Raise the white flag and keep your mouth shut.

The sonogram room isn't any easier. It's exciting knowing you're about to see a picture of your new baby, but if you don't have a rubber glove and some of that belly-jelly stuff they use for the sonogram, you'll feel out of place in there.

If it's your first baby, I should warn you, too, that the photos they hand you once it's all done might scare you just a little. No, make that more than just a little. They are definitely not the pictures you get at a photography studio. The proportions tend to look a little odd, and you might even find yourself wondering if your wife is about to give birth to something *not of this world.*

Top Ten Baby Names When the Mom Chooses

10. Preston
9. Theodore
8. John
7. Tyler
6. George
5. Harold
4. Harvey
3. Chancelor
2. Timothy
1. Harrison

Top Ten Baby Names When the Dad Chooses

10. Brett Favre
9. Crutcher
8. Brock
7. Earnhardt
6. Uriah
5. Ted
4. Buck
3. Sam
2. Brick
1. Killer

What's worse is when you show this photo around to your friends and relatives, and they all tell you how much he or she "looks just like you." Comments like that can wreak havoc on your self-esteem and send you off to the mirror to try to see the resemblance. But don't worry—your baby will be just fine!

If, however, the sonogram reveals your little one is already wearing a soccer outfit, now, *that* would be cause for concern.

Grading on the DNA Scale

We're both for education. If you bring children into this world, then *you* need to provide for them an education. But parent-teacher meetings can destroy your sense of parental worthiness faster than almost anything else. In fact, I (Rick) think some teachers have contests among themselves to see how quickly they can shatter a parent's (usually the dad's) sense of self-worth.

I have come to expect that on parent-teacher meeting night, everything our children are doing wrong will somehow be turned on me. Never mind that I have some good qualities that our offspring could very well have picked up from my side of the family; the meeting will not go down that way. Mainly that's because I'm bumping up against my wife's record of being an outstanding student and a brilliant woman. I was a C student (my football number was even 75). I got by in school on my wit and my ability to wing anything.

So if there is a complaint about how one of our children is acting, both Sherri and the teacher will look over in my direction. I can remember sitting in more than my share of parent-teacher meetings and hearing things like:

Teacher: *Your child seems to have a hard time paying attention, and he talks a lot to those around him.* (This is accompanied by a knowing look from my wife, and on more than one occasion, a finger discreetly pointing at me when she didn't think I was looking.)

Teacher: *Your child seems to think that being funny in class is going to take him somewhere.*
Me: *I have no comment.*

Teacher: *Your child knows everything about football and hunting, but seems lost on subtraction.*
Me: *And your point is?*

Teacher: *Your child's answer to what makes a country communist is* soccer.

Teacher: *Your child says the TV is just radio with pictures and it will never last.*

Teacher: *Your child wore a short-sleeved shirt—with the sleeves rolled up—to school today and asked me if I had tickets to the gun show. Can you explain?*

Teacher: *Your child begged a classmate to pull his finger.*

Teacher: *Your child thinks Shakespeare has a Southern accent.*

Teacher: *Your child has been taking the other kids' food at lunchtime. What do you have to say about that?*
Me: *No comment.*

Teacher: *Your child said he did not have his homework because liberal Democrats took it away with his freedom.*
Me: *Pull my finger.*

United We Stand,
Divided We Blame Dad

It's important for a couple to present a unified front when dealing with the children. If you are belittling, disrespecting, and negating toward Dad every time he tries to interject his opinion into a matter, you are sending a damaging signal to your children.

Contrary to what some television shows and women activists would have you believe, dads are not doofuses. The majority of dads are a positive influence on their children and have both love and life lessons to impart to them. Dads aren't always right, just as moms aren't always right. If you and your spouse can act as a unit, bringing both perspectives to the table, you'll go a long way toward bringing peace to your home.

To further prove our point, here is a list of the times we were right, and our wives were wrong, as well as those times when we were wrong, and our wives were right.

We Were Right: They didn't need that perm.
They Were Right: Four bowls of chili was too much.
We Were Right: Credit cards are not our friends. Leave home
   without them.

They Were Right: We really should have kept the windows rolled up at the Wild Animal Safari.

We Were Right: Matchmaking your friends isn't always a good idea.

They Were Right: There really wasn't enough room to park in that parking space.

We Were Right: We did too make it through the intersection on that yellow light.

They Were Right: We made it on the yellow light, but the fire truck had the right of way.

We Were Right: It's going to be the best fireworks display ever.

They Were Right: The fireworks probably did get too close to the patio.

We Were Right: Fried turkey is the best.

They Were Right: It's not a good idea to drop frozen *anything* into a vat of volcanic oil.

We Were Right: See? We're in Chicago, and we didn't even need a map to get here!

They Were Right: But we were headed to Cleveland!

We Were Right: We need to cut the fat out of the budget.

They Were Right: You need to cut the fat out of your diet.

We Were Right: See? We always knew we'd get married.

They Were Right: The mullet really did need to go.

Mama, Don't Let Your Babies Grow Up to Be Puddin' Heads

This subject comes up a lot in discussions around the campfire and at the office and at church and at football games. In fact, it comes up so often that we know it's a concern in the hearts and minds of a good percentage of husbands. What is it? *The blatant puddinization of our sons by our wives.*

There, we've said it. We know this might be controversial, but the problem needs to be put out there. Too many men have shared their feelings about this with us, as well as with other men. It's high time the women heard it—or read it. Our wives have been making puddin' heads out of our sons, and we've stood by and allowed it to happen for far too long!

Don't misunderstand us. We're not saying that all mothers are doing this. We're not even saying that the mothers who are doing this are doing it intentionally. We're just saying that it is happening, and we husbands have a growing concern over the matter.

I (Bubba) recall a certain incident at our home that will perfectly illustrate our point. One evening after dinner, my son Hunter and I started pitching a ball back and forth in the yard. He was about three at the time, and he was clearly enjoying this wonderful father-son moment.

I'd toss the ball to him, and he'd try to catch it. Then he'd throw it back to me. That's all there was to it, but it was a scene worthy of a *Saturday Evening Post* cover.

Now, I should clarify that it was a Nerf ball. For that handful of people on the planet who don't know what a Nerf ball is, it is basically like tossing a sponge around. The ball was hardly heavy enough to throw at all, but it was the perfect ball for a game of toss with a three-year-old.

So there I was, pitching this ball to my son, and it was going so well that I decided to step it up a little bit. Up until that moment, I had been throwing the ball underhand to him and he had been catching it pretty good. But then I decided to make things a little more interesting. I backed up a little bit and whipped one right to him. It was no ninety-mile-an-hour pitch; it was more like a sidearm kind of throw to him, like how you'd throw a ball from shortstop to first base. Granted, it was a little harder than what he had been used to up to that point, but did I mention *it was a sponge*?

Well, the ball hit him square in the arm, and after standing there looking at me for a few seconds, he whimpered a bit; then that little mouth started turning south, and before I could say, "Hey, it was just a sponge, little guy," he whipped around and ran crying to his momma! He jumped right up on her lap, and she wrapped her arms around him, then turned to me and said, "You're throwing the ball too hard!"

Now I ask you, can you imagine an umpire saying that to Greg Maddux? Of course not. It was only a sponge! Did I mention that? *A sponge!*

So I called a time-out to express my dissatisfaction with the call.

"Betty, honey, it's just a sponge. Even if I had wanted to, how hard could I possibly toss a sponge?"

Betty, who before becoming a mother had generally been fair, was now clearly guilty of placing blame where it didn't belong. I had done nothing wrong, so far on that day anyway. But the story was now being spun to make it look like I was the notorious Sponge Killer that the police had been looking for. The more Betty tried to console three-year-old Hunter, the more I feared that my wife had joined the ranks of so many other mothers today who are turning their sons into puddin' heads.

For those of you who are still having trouble understanding the problem here, let me explain further. *It was a sponge!* Sponges can't exactly rocket through the air. That's why you seldom see them used in a combat situation. You won't hear of the Defense Department ordering up another shipment of sponges during wartime. It's not considered a lethal weapon. I hadn't even thrown it all that hard, anyway. Yes, it was a little harder than I had been throwing it. I've already admitted to that, your honor. But for a sponge, that's not so threatening. On a scale of one to ten, a sponge doesn't even register. It's not a weapon of mass destruction. There was no reason for the tears that were now welling up in Hunter's eyes.

"Look what you did to him!" she said, puckering up in that sympathetic sort of pucker moms are so good at. "He's crying."

Of course, he was crying. That's what happens during the puddinization process. First it starts out as a whimper, then a full-blown cry, and then Mom throws in a "Come here, you poor little thing," more tears follow from both of them, and finally a "What was Daddy thinking?"

I had to defend myself.

"This is clearly *your* fault, Betty. You've been babying him too much. He's turning into a little puddin' head now, and it's all because of you."

I would have said more—I wanted to—but I had to duck the sponge being hurled in my direction.

I stand my ground on this issue, though. And dads all across America are standing with me. We can't be babying our sons if we want them to grow up in this world and be successful. Throughout their lives, a lot of sponges are going to be thrown at them. And perhaps even more hurtful things. They need to know how to survive. They need to learn that they can take a hit and keep on going. Whenever a batter gets hit by a pitch, he doesn't get sent to the bench to rest it off. He walks it off, all the way to first base. He's encouraged to stay in the game and to keep on going.

That's what our sons need to do, and our daughters, too, for that matter. They need to learn they can "walk" things off. They need to know they can survive the blow of a Nerf football.

I'm not saying our children don't need a mother's comfort. Of course they do. We're simply pointing out that there has to be balance. Sons and daughters need a dad, too. That's why God made mothers and fathers different. We need the qualities that each one brings to our lives.

Growing up, my (Rick's) dad was the enforcer at our house. My mom would beat down the little fires that would erupt throughout the day. But if a flame ever got to licking up a little too much, then it was Dad's turn. Dad was the one who handled the infernos.

As soon as my dad's gold Chevrolet pickup hit that gravel driveway up to our home, the sound would reverberate inside the entire house. Especially if it was an Enforcer Day, when Mom had said, "Just wait until your father gets home!"

My brother and I shared a room, and we would start bawling in anticipation of the encounter long before Dad ever got that truck parked. My father had established some consistency over the years, so we knew that if he was going to be called upon to put out a fire, that fire had no chance whatsoever.

Maybe that's what's wrong with this generation of fathers. We've turned everything over to Mom. Or in some instances, Mom has overstepped and overrode us on so many things that we've just given up. But it's time we as husbands and dads take back our position in the household and do our part to raise men and women who know how to "walk to the base." The world doesn't need more players being carried off the field due to sponge-inflicted injuries. Victim mentality is already epidemic in this country. Let's do our part to start reversing some of this.

After all, if a sponge can bring us to our knees, we're all in deep trouble.

We're Not the Enemy

We don't want a sponge to bring our sons to their knees, and we don't want to always be the bad guy in the child-rearing process either.

Despite how you've seen us portrayed in movies, despite decades of Mom's "Wait till your father gets home!" comments, despite therapy groups and sarcastic Father's Day cards, we feel we must clear up a popular misconception: Dads are not nearly as concerned about discipline as we have been made out to be. In fact, the threat of "Wait till your father gets home" was simply a strategy conceived by women to get their children to mind *them,* not Dad.

In most situations, the kids themselves do not see Dad's arrival home as a serious threat. They usually can't wait until he gets home so he can repeal, at least from their perception, the excessive sentence that Mom just handed down ("You're grounded for life!"), or at least get it significantly reduced.

Don't get us wrong, ladies. This is not about undercutting Mom's authority. We're just tired when we get home. And believe it or not, we're happy to see our kids. We don't want to walk through the door and immediately start handing out discipline.

So when we respond with something like, "Mom said you have to go to your room? Well, then, yes, you're going to have to do that—

right after we watch this cool movie I just rented," try not to take it personally.

If you want to know the truth, most of the trouble that kids get into with Dad is due to the fact that they have upset Mom with their infraction, and now Dad has to deal with an upset wife. Because of this, someone is going to pay dearly.

I (Rick) remember learning this rule of Daddy Discipline (DD) around the time I turned seventeen. That was the first time my dad let the age-old DD secret slip out. I had gotten into some kind of trouble with Mom, and without thinking, Dad said—no, he begged—"Son, you are killing me here. This getting your mom upset has got to stop."

At that moment, something inside of me clicked. *Wait a minute*, I thought. *Dad doesn't really care that I left the car dirty when Mom needed it. He's only upset because Mom is upset, and now he has to deal with her anger.*

Instinctively, I already knew that *"Wait till your father gets home"* didn't carry the weight that my mother believed it did. Unless, of course, I had really done something bad, and then I got what I had coming.

But Mom used the "Wait till your father gets home" card so often, it had started to lose its power anyway. And once I learned the DD secret, the whole picture changed. I could sympathize with Dad's predicament, and I tried going a little easier on him and helping him out by listening to Mom.

So now that we have established where most dads are coming from and how a good majority of them have been unjustly made out to be the bad guy in our minds, the following provides further clarification on the matter:

Differences Between Mom Discipline and Dad Discipline

Infraction: Running in the house

Mom: "Stop running this instant! Someone is going to get hurt!"

Dad: "Hey, kids, don't run in front of the TV."

Infraction: Eating dirt

Mom: "Spit that out of your mouth right now! I'm going to call Poison Control, while you go wash your mouth out!"

Dad: "Awww, he'll learn."

Infraction: Eating candy for supper

Mom: "Absolutely not! You'll ruin your dinner. You need to eat a meat, a starch, something green, and a healthy dessert like fruit."

Dad: "Hey, let me try that. I've never put M&M's in ice cream before."

Infraction: Not wearing a jacket

Mom: "Don't you go out that door without a jacket on! You'll catch a cold!"

Dad: "Nah, you don't have to bring a jacket. That way, when we play football in the yard, you won't have to keep track of it."

Infraction: Not making your bed

Mom: "You're not leaving your room until you make your bed!"

Dad: "Go ahead and leave it unmade. You're just going to mess it up again tonight anyway."

Infraction: Picking out the wrong clothes to wear

Mom: "March right back upstairs this instant! You will not go out the door wearing something that doesn't match."

Dad: "Hey, buddy. That Looney Tunes shirt looks great with your Superman tights. Go get the cape!"

Infraction: Dropping food on floor

Mom: "You're going to have to throw it away now. Who knows how many germs just got on it?"

Dad: "Has the five-second rule ever really been disproved?"

Infraction: Spilling a glass of milk on the table

Mom: "That wouldn't have happened if you were paying attention!"

Dad: "Quick! Go get the cat!"

Infraction: Throwing a ball in the house

Mom: "Stop that before you knock something over!"

Dad: "Hey! I'm wide open! Quick! Throw it and I'll go in for the touchdown!"

Infraction: Disobeying Mom

Mom: "Don't you even think about it!"

Dad: "Hey, if I can't get away with that, neither can you!"

Mixed Marriages

Betty Lou and I (Bubba) have a mixed marriage. She is a workout guru, even to the point of teaching aerobics classes at our church. I am the polar opposite of that. I picked up an aerobics tape from the sofa once, but it was only so I could lie down.

When Betty first started teaching aerobics, I was as supportive as any husband could be. Right after she made her announcement in our Sunday school class that she would be teaching the exercise sessions, I stood up and said, "Just think, people, now Betty can do for you what she's done for me!"

We had some people almost choke on the donut they were eating when I said that. (We have a snack ministry in our Sunday school class, which, when I think about it in hindsight, seems counter-productive to the aerobics class announcement. But I digress.)

When Betty first started teaching the class, she was very excited. She made sure the workout outfits were just right, and she started shaving her legs twice a day. She wanted everything to be perfect.

I'll have to confess, I do enjoy watching my wife work out. Betty is one fine-looking woman. In my opinion, she's one step ahead of exercise guru Denise Austin. When Betty works out, I get reminded once again of how very lucky I am. So naturally, I've supported this new endeavor of hers 100 percent.

There is a twist to this story, however. It happened one day not long after Betty had begun the class, and it proves that just because she's an aerobics instructor does not mean my *own* athletic skills should be underestimated. Our son, Hunter, who was four at the time, wanted me to go outside and play with him, so I obliged and out we went.

"Daddy, I want to hit the baseball," he said excitedly.

We got the tee out, and he hit the baseball a few times. But as you know, at four years of age, kids' attention spans are short, so they don't stay with anything very long. He got bored and said, "Daddy, I want to throw a football now."

We got the football out and tossed it around a little bit. Before long, he remembered another sport. "Daddy, I want to go shoot basketball," he said.

At that time, we had a basket that cranked down low so Hunter could use a regular basketball to play. He enjoyed this a lot more than playing with the little plastic basket that was more his size.

So we played basketball for a while, but then he got tired of that.

"I don't know what else to do, Hunter," I said, trying to save some wear and tear on heart and lungs. "We've played baseball, football, basketball—the big three. What else is there?"

The disappointed look on Hunter's face convinced me to go back into the garage and pilfer around to see what else I could find. But before I tell you what I did find, I should mention that my garage has been called by some "the mad scientist lab." And with good cause. The garage is my workshop. I keep everything in there, everything short of a Frankenstein monster. But I do have the plans.

Anyway, I saw this unopened box in the corner of the garage and wasn't sure what was in it, but figured I'd go over and check it out.

Since nothing moved when I opened the lid, I went ahead and started looking through it.

The box turned out to be a sampling of soccer equipment that a friend of mine had dropped off one day in an effort to try to lure Hunter into the sport. There were stickers in there, a little soccer ball, an outfit, a net, and even a trophy. Everything that you could possibly need to play soccer was in that box.

As we started looking through it, Hunter began to get more and more interested in all the equipment. Before I knew it, I was taking the net out of the box, along with some metal posts and knee pads, and saying to myself, *What would it hurt if we played a little bit?* We had already tried the big three sports; what could possibly be wrong with throwing soccer into the mix?

What I didn't realize was that the innocent-looking box I had opened in my garage that day wasn't just a box of soccer equipment; it was Pandora's box. But I naively plunged full speed ahead. I put the goal together out in the yard and then started kicking the soccer ball around with Hunter. I convinced myself that nobody was going to see me. Rick was nowhere near my house at that moment. There were no neighbors with digital cameras or camcorders to get this private, family moment circulating around on the Internet, so what could it possibly hurt?

But I had underestimated the power of Pandora. What began as innocent fun quickly turned into something bigger than both of us. First, I started thinking that Hunter wasn't running fast enough, and I started chasing him, just to make the game more interesting. I kicked the ball into the net. My cheering woke up Kaitlyn, who was two at the time.

Before long Betty appeared in the doorway, with baby Kaitlyn on her hip.

"Hey, what are you doing?" she asked, surprised to see the soccer equipment, but I trusted her to keep the incident between us.

"Well, we've played all the other sports," I said. "I thought we'd give this a try. We're just knocking the ball around a bit."

Betty watched Hunter kick the ball a few times, and then she said, "You know, I think he needs to work on his defense. I'll tell you what: I'll play goalie, and it'll be me and Hunter against you."

Now, at that point I should have known better. For years it has been our family's stand that soccer is a Communist plot; therefore, we have never allowed our kids to play the sport. (Please don't write me letters about this. We *know* soccer has nothing to do with Communism. As far as we know, neither Stalin nor Khrushchev was ever seen publicly in shorts and knee pads. We are taking creative license here.)

We don't believe in the sport, but there I was, being challenged by my wife the aerobics instructor, to a game of soccer.

To make the competition more interesting, Betty said she would be playing goalie with Kaitlyn on her hip! Personally, I think that was a ploy for me to spot her some points, but it didn't work. I'm a very competitive human being. Betty knew that when she made the challenge. She had to know that I was going to give it everything I've got, baby on board or no baby on board.

Hunter couldn't have been more excited about the challenge. He got in the defensive position and then watched as I kicked the ball down the yard with all my might. It was a good, straight kick, and I took off running after it. In all modesty, I have to say that I ran right past Hunter. He couldn't even get close to me. I was leaving that four-year-old in the dust! He couldn't take it and broke down right there in the middle of the yard. He just stopped and stood there with his legs spread apart and started crying. My heart went out to him, but I took advantage of the moment and kicked the ball between his legs, and then picked it up on the other side.

With my confidence now soaring, I continued moving down the yard toward the lovely Betty Lou, who was waiting to take me down and vindicate Hunter. But I was still high from getting the ball past Hunter, and I thought, *Well, I'll just kick it by Betty, too.*

Bad decision.

In the spirit of the moment, I guess I got a little carried away and kicked the ball a little harder than I meant to. Okay, a *lot* harder than I meant to. I was trying to kick it *around* Betty, but I kicked it right at her. As soon as it left my foot, I knew I was in trouble. I could see where it was heading and thought to myself, *Oh, boy, have I made a big mistake!*

There was nothing I could do about it at that point. It was airborne and heading straight for her thighs! When it made contact, it sounded like bacon sizzling.

Betty soon made a few sounds of her own, which are difficult to put into print—not profanity, just gibberish that sounded an awful lot like it.

Betty set Kaitlyn down and then began to run around the yard like something had stung her. This, of course, upset both Kaitlyn and Hunter, who didn't understand what was wrong with Mommy. When Betty sat down and started rubbing her legs, I went over and immediately apologized for what I had so innocently done. I'm telling you, soccer balls have their own agenda. It is an evil sport. I had tampered with the dark side, and this is what happened. I had let my guard down.

I gave Betty the win. It was the only fair thing to do. And I packed up all the soccer equipment and put it back in the corner of the garage.

Pandora's box is safely sealed once again.

School Programs

I f you're a parent of school-aged children, you already know what the PTO is. If you don't have any children, allow me (Rick) to explain.

The PTO is what the old PTA used to be. What the difference is, I can't tell you, but primarily it is an organization of parents who come together from time to time to discuss how they can improve their kids' school. If you've ever bought a chocolate bar from a third grader, chances are the PTO was behind it.

The bottom line is this—and we're being brutally honest here—most parents are not all that fired up about going to the PTO meetings. Can we just say that? Not much PTO business could be called exciting. They hand the budget to you, and you cast your vote; beyond that, it's pretty boring stuff. Besides, most of the same information you'd get at the meeting arrives in the flyers your kids bring home. We know we probably should be more interested, since it's about our children's school and their education, but we just don't have the time for more boring meetings.

The PTO knows this and has come up with what we think is an ingenious marketing scheme to get more parents to show up at their meetings. They've started planning a cute program featuring the kids for each meeting, and that's how they trick you into attending. Once you're there, they do their PTO business before the entertainment. Brilliant!

Granted, it's just the parents of the kids in the presentation attending these meetings, but it's still about fifty more people than would have been there otherwise.

For this one particular PTO meeting where our kids Brandi and Blake were going to be featured in the cute presentation, Sherri and I had promised to attend. But let the record show that I always try to give Sherri an out on things like this. I always tell her that I'll capture it on video, so if she would prefer to stay home with the younger kids, that would be fine.

At this time, it was our twenty-month-old son, Brooks Burgess, who goes by the nicknames "Rambo" and "Big Love," who presented cause for concern. It's not always easy to corral a twenty-month-old baby, so I wanted Sherri to know I was cool with her staying home with him. Nothing against the boy, but twenty months is twenty months. At that age, they don't sit still at all. And this kid had lungs you would not believe. He loved screaming as loud as he could, just to hear himself. I knew that if he got into a room with any kind of echo, we could kiss our eardrums good-bye.

Rambo had also learned, as all kids do, that he could pretty much get whatever he wanted if he embarrassed us enough. He had us over a barrel whenever we were out in public. We'd try anything just to get him to stop making a scene. I'm not talking tantrum here; he was just really loud.

Now, if you're like my mom, you don't let that bother you. But most of us can't do that. It's easy to claim, "Why, if that were my kid, I'd—" or, "Hey, don't put up with that. Don't let 'em run you." You can talk like that all you want, but until you've been dealt that card yourself, it doesn't mean anything. When you're there, when everyone in the grocery store, church, or library is hearing him, believe me, you just want it to be over.

Unfortunately the kid knows this.

Being a typical mom, though, Sherri wasn't about to stay home with Rambo and miss the program. After all, Brandi and Blake were playing famous Alabamians in the play. Would Dustin Hoffman be the actor he is today if his mom or dad had missed his school plays? Who knows, but Sherri didn't want to take that chance.

When we arrived at the school, I rushed to find the best place to angle the camcorder. Blake (Boomer) was playing John Pelham, and Brandi was portraying a young girl from Alabama who had gone on to become a missionary in Africa.

Once the PTO business was over and the show started, Rambo began running low on patience. He was being a little rambunctious, but he wasn't totally unmanageable. Sherri, though, could see that he was distracting me a little, so she came over and took him down to the front row where he could be with her and maybe walk around a little.

In the interest of honesty, I admit that as soon as Sherri said she was taking Rambo, I breathed a sigh of relief. I was released from the responsibility of watching him and could now concentrate solely on my duties as cameraman. Translation: *From that point on, it was all on her.* Knowing Rambo was in Mom's very capable hands, I went back to my videotaping.

Until . . .

I heard a familiar *shriek*. The play was going full throttle, and there it was. A shriek that I had heard a hundred times before at home and in every building in Birmingham with an echo. It was loud, and I could see the other parents looking around to see where it had come from.

We ducked our heads, and I think I saw Sherri even scoot a few inches away from him.

Rambo still hadn't noticed that Brandi and Blake were in the play, so the shriek wasn't about that. He just thought the echo was cool.

I knew if he got sight of his brother and sister, it would all be over. So I started wondering about putting blinders on him. I kid you not, and if you think that's cruel, you don't have kids. I contemplated taking some flash cards and attaching them with a rubber band to the sides of his face, like you would to a stallion. I'd have made sure the rubber band wasn't too tight, of course. But I knew that if Rambo saw Brandi and Blake (who weren't even onstage—they were at his level on the gym floor), there was no way he would remain in his seat.

Disaster loomed, and I knew it. After that first shriek, Rambo got that look in his eyes that said, *Hey, that was loud.* That look was immediately followed by another that said, *Hey, I think I'll do it again!*

I wanted to intervene and help Sherri, but I was at my picture-taking post and couldn't leave. Besides, Sherri had already made the rookie mistake of telling Rambo that he could go ahead and run out as far as a black tile on the gym floor, as long as he came right back.

But Rambo wanted more.

On one of his advances out to the black tile, he locked in and saw his brother and sister. All rules of engagement were immediately out, and Rambo now advanced right smack into the middle of the program.

He ran up to Blake and Brandi and was now one of the great Alabamians. He started singing along with the other kids, and of course, the crowd thought it was great. They loved every minute of it.

I'm not sure the teachers were too excited about it, though. They had worked hard to get the program together and hadn't foreseen Rambo's stage debut.

Because I was trapped up in my photographer's spot, getting all of this on video, the task of rescuing our offspring fell to Sherri, who now had to get up and step into the middle of the program to get Rambo off the stage. But Rambo apparently wanted a bigger role and started wrestling with her and pitching a fit. Meanwhile, my camera was rolling and getting it all—Rambo's antics, Sherri's face, the look of horror on all the teachers' faces.

Is it worth $10,000 on *America's Funniest Videos*? Maybe. Especially the expression on Sherri's face when she looked up toward the camera with the *Why aren't you down here helping me?* face that every husband has seen a thousand times.

When we got home that night, I asked Sherri if she'd like to see the film, you know, to critique it like they do after a football game.

"Maybe you'll see some things you might do differently next time," I said. "You seemed to come in a little high on that one move. And you might want to work on your blocking. Your defensive moves could use some work, too. And—"

At that point, Sherri cut in. I don't really know what all she said because she was talking so fast and she seemed a bit, well, *agitated* with me. But that's okay. The camera was still rolling, so I can play it back later and have her give me a play-by-play of it in the privacy of our home.

And maybe even at future PTO special events.

Is There a Helpmate in the House?

There is no disputing the fact that men and women face illness differently. Ever since Adam told Eve that he felt a chill coming on (right after they both ate the forbidden fruit), and Eve said, "Me too. But go get your own leaf; these three are mine!" men have been left to fend for themselves when they're feeling a little under the weather.

After the Fall, it immediately became painfully obvious that our wives were far better suited to handle the aches and pains of everyday life. And even more—like the pain of birthing children. Childbirth is not an easy thing to do. We men would never be able to accomplish that. At the very first birth pang, we would be ringing the nurse for the epidural and offering to buy a round of the medication for everyone else in the room, too.

That being the case, you would think that our wives would take pity on us. We can't help it that we are the weaker sex when it comes to pain. It's how we're internally wired. We men can go into battle and fight bravely to the death. But let us get a sinus infection, and we're laid out flat on our backs like a Thanksgiving turkey.

But does anyone offer us any pity, ask how we're doing, or bring us a cold towel for our brow? Oftentimes, our beloved wives, whom we distinctly heard promise to "love, honor, and cherish" us "in sickness and in health," will refuse to attend to our needs even though our fever is running a full 99 degrees. They won't bring us an extra blanket if we get chilled from the refrigerated soda we asked for just before the blanket. They won't fluff our pillows, not even the ones we took from their side of the bed.

If you ask me (Rick), I don't believe Florence Nightingale ever really existed. I think she was a figment of a man's imagination, conjured up while he was trying to overcome a stomach virus. What man among us doesn't dream of someone catering to our every need when we're sick? I'm not talking about anything beyond someone getting us that blanket we've asked for or a cool glass of water. We wouldn't even care if she looked like Aunt Bea. In fact, we'd probably like her to look like Aunt Bea. And cook like her. It's the caretaking we're after.

But back to reality.

The women in my life have never cut me any slack when I'm sick, beginning with my mother. I could have been burning up with fever, but I still had to get up and go to school. If I were on life support, she would have paid my brother Greg a dollar to push the gurney to my homeroom and leave me there. She was an angel of no mercy, as she put it, "for my own good."

Don't get me wrong, I know my mother loves me. She just didn't want to raise a puddin' head.

This kind of treatment has continued with my wife, Sherri. To me, Sherri is a lot more like General Patton than Florence Nightingale.

Aunt Bea, where are you?

Bubba and I have often tried to decide which one of us has the least merciful wife when it comes to caring for us when we are ill, and we always come up with the same answer—it's a toss-up.

Once, when I was in bed with one of those stomach bugs that has you crawling to the bathroom, moaning endless promises to God that if He would just make you feel better, you would double your tithe, never miss church, and stop after the third plate of meat loaf, I discovered just how alone I was in my pain.

After my third visit to the porcelain throne, I dragged myself back to the bed and began to think how good some ice-cold Sprite would feel on my upset stomach. And perhaps a few saltine crackers, too. I was only trying to get something to stay on my stomach, but since I didn't have the strength to crawl to the kitchen myself, I called to my wife.

"Honey, Angel of Kindness, Sherri, would you please bring me a glass of Sprite and some crackers?"

I was in a dehydrated stupor, so my voice was weak, but I knew she heard me.

"I'm busy," Sherri replied. "You'll need to go get them yourself."

At first I thought, *Oh no! My fever is so high that I am now hearing voices! I could swear I just heard my beloved wife, or someone who sounds like her, tell me to go get them myself.*

Not trusting my own ears, I asked again, "Honey, sweetness, love of my life, could you bring me up some Sprite and crackers?"

The Sherri impersonator returned. It sounded a lot like my wife, but this woman was much louder and firmer. "We don't have any Sprite," the voice said. "You'll have to go to the store at the bottom of the hill and get it."

Considering the strength it had just taken for me to crawl to the bathroom and back, I couldn't believe what she was now asking of me. If I couldn't have made it to the kitchen, how could I possibly make it to the store? I was sick, but Sherri was the one who was delirious! What happened to our "in sickness and in health"? To our "till death (which I was surely on the brink of) do us part"? Apparently all that went out the window in my hour of need. Not that she was purposely trying to be mean. She was simply being detached, which she must have thought was for my own good.

But Aunt Bea would have gone to get the Sprite.

I (Bubba) was in a similar situation once. I had gotten sick to the point that I thought I was going to dangerously dehydrate. So I told Betty that I needed to go to the hospital. Betty, being a nurse, disagreed. In spite of the fact that the virus was giving me a Kermit complexion that was clashing with the drapes, Betty held to her guns.

"You'll be fine," she said.

Now, I have no doubt that Betty had my best interest in mind, too, but from my weakened state, I had to whimper, "Hon, if you don't take me to the hospital, I will be forced to call 911 for a pickup."

Betty didn't budge. She simply walked over and unplugged the phone and took it out of the room so I couldn't call for help. Like Rick, my fever was well over 99 degrees. I believe it was 99.3.

But like Sherri, Betty told me that I needed to battle my way back to health on my own, while she tended to the house. She also made a few references to Patton, and like I said, she was "doing it all for my own good." But unlike Patton, she didn't slap me.

Still, I think you can see that when it comes to caretaking, we consider it a toss-up as to which one of our spouses is tougher. When the gift of mercy was handed out, both our wives neglected to get in that line.

And don't think that our wives are simply paying us back for our neglect of them when they are sick. No, no, no. That is not the case at all! Whenever our wives are ill, we try our best to be dutiful husbands and take care of the precious gifts that God has given us. We bring them water whenever they ask for it—as soon as the football game we're watching takes a commercial break. We bring them a wet hand towel for their fevered brows—right after we're through using it in the shower. We take them hot chicken soup—whatever's left over from the can we had with our lunch. We are helpmates in the fullest sense of the word. So it's clearly not a payback situation.

But caring for your wife when she's under the weather can get tricky. Not only will she not appreciate what you do for her, but you run the risk of landing in the "no-win" zone of getting on her nerves.

"Bubba, do you have to stir that soup so loudly?"

"Must you lose so many feathers when you're fluffing my pillow?"

"This water has only three ice cubes in it, honey. I asked for four."

Okay, maybe there is a hint of exaggeration there, but I do recall one particular time that will perfectly illustrate my point of how uneven the sickbed treatment can be between a husband and a wife.

One Valentine's Day, I got so sick it felt like Cupid had missed my heart completely and hit my upper intestine instead. I was driving home from work and decided that I would stop by the pharmacy and pick up some medicine first, so I could go straight to bed when I got there.

On my way to the pharmacy, though, Betty called, and when I told her I was going to stop by to get some medicine, she lovingly convinced me that since that was going to take more time and I wasn't feeling well anyway, I should come on home and she would get the medicine for me. Supper was already on the table, and that way I could eat and go straight to bed, and leave the errand to her.

I thought to myself, *What a sweet, wonderful wife I have been blessed with.* I've always known that Betty is sweet and wonderful, but that night she was turning it up even more. I believe I even sighed at her kind offer.

But then she added, "And you wouldn't mind if while I'm out getting that, I went by the tanning bed, would you?"

What happened to my Aunt Bea? Aunt Bea doesn't go to tanning beds.

Even in my weakened state, I was starting to catch on. The tanning salon was the true underlying issue here. Not my sickness, not Betty caring for her beloved husband. The issue was *Momma needs a tan.* That was what was driving all her concern. What my wife, Betty, was really saying was, "I need you to come home and babysit so I can go to the tanning bed. Oh, and by the way, I'll swing by and pick up your medicine while I'm out."

Yes, I was onto her. Most women don't know this, but we husbands are bilingual. We speak our native tongue, but we are also fluent in wife-speak. We don't always share this knowledge with our wives, much like a secret agent hides the fact that he can speak the language of the other side. By playing dumb, he can gather more information. But it's time to let you in on our secret. We understand wife-speak. We've always understood it. *We have broken your secret code and understand the hidden meaning of every word you're saying.*

I stopped Betty dead in her tracks when I then went into our banter, the one that we have around the house periodically, when we say (very jokingly), *"Oh, it's all about you."*

"This is about you, isn't it, Betty?" I said. "It's not about sick Daddy. It's not about supper. It's not about prescriptions. It's about 'Betty needs to go to the tanning bed.'"

Knowing that I was onto her, Betty got so tickled that she broke into a fit of laughter. She was laughing so hard, she couldn't talk. She couldn't defend herself. She knew she had been caught.

"Well, I just thought—" she began between gasps for air. "I just thought—"

I cut her off at the pass. "No, no, I see. What you thought was *It's all about Betty and her tan.* But that's okay; I'll play that game. I'll come on home, and I'll try not to be in the way or anything when I get there. I'll just crawl to the sofa and then stay there and babysit the kids while you run down and get your tan."

As I hung up, I could hear Betty still laughing on the other end of the line.

So I drove straight home. I didn't stop at the pharmacy because I didn't want to interrupt her plans. That's one reason. The other one was I was enjoying finally gaining the high road. Husbands don't get to travel on the high road too often, and even when we do, our wives don't always admit seeing us there. This time I had both. I had the high road, and Betty knew I had it.

As soon as I got home, Betty, still laughing, greeted me and then headed out the door. That's one thing about wives—you can be on the high road, but it doesn't always deter their travel plans in any way.

But little did I realize that my high road was about to gain some more altitude. Betty hadn't been gone very long when I got a phone call from her.

"You're not going to believe this, Bill," she began. "I'm down here at the tanning salon, and it appears I left my wallet at the house. I have no money, no credit cards, no nothing. Looks like I can't get your prescription, after all."

Now, for the record, I'd done this sort of thing myself plenty of times, so I wasn't too upset. Without any money, she couldn't get her tan either, so we were both going to have to sacrifice. But when I said that I'd see her at home in a few, she replied, "Oh, I can still get my tan. Luckily, I've already prepaid for that. So I'll go ahead and get my tan, and then I'll see you back at home later."

That's wife-speak for *"I'm getting my tan and you're getting zip."*

I couldn't resist. "Oh . . . it's all about the tan. That's what it's about, isn't it, Betty?"

She laughed again, and then told me they were waiting for her to climb into the tanning bed, and she had to go. Now, remember, I'm burning up with fever (I believe it was 99.4), so the mere thought of someone cooking their body *on purpose* didn't make much sense to me.

I hung up the phone and then told the troops that Patton was going to be delayed.

"Sorry, Hunter, Momma's gotta get her tan. Hope she makes it back home tonight." Hunter could tell by the smirk on my face that I was kidding. But it did feel good to talk it through with someone, even if he was drinking from a sippy cup, and his own command of the English language, or wife-speak, for that matter, was limited.

When Betty finally got home that night, she was still laughing over the incident. Truly feeling bad and wanting to regain as much of the high road as possible, she said, "Look, honey, I'm going to feed the baby, and then I'll go back out and get your medicine."

It was a noble offer. But not wanting to be a bother, and protecting my beautiful wife from the outside elements, I said, "No, I don't want you out. It's late now." And it was late. It was going on seven o'clock, which everyone knows is my bedtime. "Betty," I repeated. "I don't want you out on the highway at this time of night."

Now, get this visual: I had fallen asleep on the couch, so my hair was kicked up sideways, and my eyes were droopy. I didn't have any shoes on, so hunched over, I started shuffling my way through the living room and then said, "Where are your keys, honey? I'll just go on and get the medicine myself. I think I can make it."

Betty was now laughing so hard she was begging me to stop. But I continued toward the phone and picked it up.

"What are you doing?" she asked.

"I guess I'm much too weak. I'm going to call Speedy and see if he'll pick up that prescription for me. I've got to have something, Betty. I'm dying here."

Like I said, I don't usually get to hold the high ground, and it was such a nice change, I wasn't about to let go. Meanwhile, Betty and her tan had moved into Shameville.

"I'm sorry, honey," she kept repeating. "I'm going right now."

Well, I finally did get my medicine, and I did recover. But it proves my point, doesn't it? Many of us men are left to fend for ourselves when we are ill. It's sad, but so painfully true.

Of course, when Betty's sick, like Rick does with Sherri, I always rise to the occasion. Here's a perfect illustration of that fact:

Rick and I both coach Little League baseball, and on this one particular day, we were on the field in the middle of talking to some of the team members when Sherri walked by Rick and said, "Taz is playing with Kaitlyn. And I'm off to help Betty."

Then she walked off.

So there Rick was, standing in the field, wondering if he had heard what he thought he'd heard. Then Sherri shouted back, "Betty's passed out!"

Since Betty is my wife, this made it an even more precarious situation for me. Our son Hunter was on the field, and I had already made a sporting deal with him. All he wanted to do was talk about how we were going to head to Target after the game to get the sword I had promised him if he did well.

The chant was endless.

"Hey, Daddy, Daddy . . . three points and I'm going to Target. Three points!"

Meanwhile, Betty was passed out by the stands, and I was busy fanning her. Our daughter Kaitlyn was afraid that she wasn't going to get to stay at the ball field and play with her buddies, so she began her chant.

"Daddy, can I just stay here, huh, Daddy, huh?"

"No, dear. You're five. We don't leave you unattended at the ball field. You're coming with us."

"No, I don't want to go, Daddy!"

"Daddy," Hunter broke in. *"Daddy—three! I get three and we're going to Target!"*

Beneath me, Betty was moaning, *"Just get me to the car. Just get me to the car."*

People were coming up and asking if they could help. Of course, I told them there was nothing they could do. Betty has hypoglycemia. This sort of thing has become a regular occurrence at our home. So I tried to just pass it off as a promo for our upcoming CD.

Sherri helped me get Betty to the car, and since there was a walka-thon going on that day, paramedics were already there on the site. They, too, offered their assistance; but paramedics will take a lot of tests and then send you the bill. So I said, "No it's not necessary. She's hypoglycemic; it'll pass."

"Just let us check her out," they said.

I relented, so they ran all their tests and then they gave us the diag-nosis, "Well, her blood sugar's low."

"I know," I said. "That's what I told you before you started."

After this crazy scenario, and with Betty safe in the car and Sherri with her, I returned to first base. Betty was still a little groggy, and I was worried about her; but under that kind of pressure, sometimes your brain just goes kind of wacky, and you say to yourself, *What's any of this have to do with the game?*

The team was waiting for the "all clear" signal from me, like they do after a player is carried off the field on a stretcher in football. Once you know they're going to be attended to, you go on with the game, right?

So there I was, feeling a little pressure to assure everyone that things were being taken care of and that we could all get back to a game we don't even keep score in. Our daughter Kaitlyn was running loose somewhere within the ball park fence. But I had no idea where she was. Betty was fine; I was sure of that because Sherri was with her and she had already started to come around when I left her.

So with everything sort of back in order, I was ready to play ball. Hunter was, too, and he was on fire. He hit the ball three times in a row. He couldn't have performed better. (I've learned his motivation. He's a contract man. It's all about "What's in it for me?" We had the Target deal, and so he was performing better than I could have hoped. The same Target shopping deal might have helped Betty come around sooner, but I didn't want to push it.)

It was sad, though, that Betty didn't get to see any of Hunter's baseball magic, and I felt bad about that. But I felt good that I had attended to her every need—a lot of it through Sherri, and the paramedics who about charged us a house payment, but her needs had been met in her time of crisis.

I managed to locate Kaitlyn, too, so with the baseball game over, we were finally ready to go home. On the way I told Betty about

Hunter's hits. Then I couldn't resist questioning her, "All right, Betty, cough it up. What have you been doing? Have you been eating Kit Kats again?"

Betty broke out in a sweat, a different one than she had been sweating before. This was guilt-induced sweat. She admitted that, yes, she'd been sampling the kids' Halloween candy, which hypoglycemic people are not supposed to do. But Betty has a sweet tooth, so when she gets to eating candy, she can't stop and eventually will drop like a light. So it looks like Betty's days of going trick-or-treating with the kids are over. If I can't trust her to stay out of the candy bags, what else can I do?

Oh, and as for her tan . . . that's still good, too.

Hospital Visits

While we're on the subject of "in sickness and in health," there is nowhere that the difference between a man and a woman is more apparent than when one of them has to be admitted to a hospital.

Women can go into a hospital, deliver a nine-pound baby, and then go back home a couple of days later. Men consider it more of a vacation, so much so that other men tend to be a little jealous when one of their buddies gets to go.

I (Rick) went to visit Bubba when he was in the hospital for a sports injury, and I have to admit I was a little jealous. Come on, guys, you know that sort of thing happens. As long as the condition isn't too serious, you get a green light on everything while you're in a hospital. People are constantly calling you up to see if they can do anything for you.

"Hey, man, can we bring you some ribs?"

"Well, they're checking my cholesterol again in the morning. They said it was a little high. So make them dry, with a little Cajun rub."

If you're like most men, a hospitalization is almost as good as a season pass to your favorite sports team. People do things for you that they would never do for you otherwise.

Helpful People: *"You want the wife and me to go to your house and clean? I'm sure Sherri could use a little help while you're away."*

You: *"Yeah, that'd be great. You don't mind? Oh, and if you'd like, go ahead and get started on the new deck. I'd help, but as you know, I'm in the hospital."*

Helpful People: *"You want us to watch your kids for the next three weeks?"*

You: *"Really? Could you? That's so kind of you because, as you know, I'm in the hospital."*

Helpful People: *"Do you need any help with the medical expenses?"*

You: *"Thanks. I've got insurance, but there is a new fishing boat that I've had my eye on. It'd sure perk me up, you know, since I'm in the hospital."*

It doesn't stop once you're home either. You can keep on milking it until your family and friends finally catch on.

"I really should get up and help you around the house, Sherri. . . . Oh, no, wait, oh my . . . I'm feeling a little light-headed. Better get back to bed. As you know, I just got out of the hospital."

"Could you turn on the TV and hand me the remote? I'd get it myself, but I've been in the hospital."

"My face feels a little warm, Sherri. Could you get me a cool towel? And go ahead and take away the blanket I asked for. I don't think I need it anymore. A glass of water would be nice, though. Remember, I just got out of the hospital and . . ."

Well, you get the idea. Depending on your performance, you could actually have your wife *ordering* you back to bed to get some rest! (So she can get some too!) But it's great—guilt-free pampering! And all you had to do was get one of your vital organs removed or have some other medical procedure done. In many cases, it's more than worth it.

Bubba's hospital stay was like a fun zone for him. He had the television going; people were bringing him snacks; there were cards and flowers all over the place. He could even adjust his bed however he wanted it. And if he ever wanted to be alone, all he had to do was pull the curtain around his bed. You can't do that at home. When the kids are driving you crazy, or your wife is after you to do some chores around the house, you can't just pull a curtain around yourself and block them all out. (Although that is something home decorators might want to start including in their designs.)

From my vantage point, Bubba had it made. So naturally, I was jealous. He could lie there and sleep all day. Or watch whatever shows he wanted to on TV. He didn't have to watch cartoons or soap operas or *Oprah*. He had control of the remote, and as long as they didn't put another patient in his room, he was king of his domain. He didn't have to worry about reading or answering his e-mails, either. Or checking his voice mail. Or picking up the kids from school. Or helping with their homework. Or stopping by the store and picking up something for dinner.

So yes, I was jealous. But since I don't have any surgeries planned in the foreseeable future, I guess my pampering will have to wait. Besides, I'm still trying to decide which vital organ I could do without.

Female in Hospital	Male in Hospital
"My heart feels like it's racing."	"Could you turn the television about a quarter inch to the right?"
"The contractions are one minute apart."	"Could you tuck the blanket in around my feet?"
"Can I have something for the pain?"	"The electrical storm's messing up the reception on the TV. Do you happen to have the score for the 'Bama game?"
"Should my incision be oozing like this?"	"Got any chips and dip?"
"The pain in my abdomen is back."	"If I order pizza, should they just drop it off at the nurse's station?"
"I can't eat a thing. You can go ahead and take away my meal tray."	"If the patient they just wheeled out of here isn't coming back, could I have his pudding?"
"My IV drip is backing up."	"Does this drip come in any other flavors—like, say, barbeque?"
"It feels like the room is spinning."	"Is there a gym here?"

"Do you have my blood test results?"

"Would you fax something for me?"

"I think my dressing needs changing."

"I think my gown is missing the back."

Leverage

When my (Rick's) family goes on vacation now, we tend to need a much bigger car than the ones we have in our driveway. With all the kids, along with their suitcases and toys, and the teenagers, with all their electronics, things tend to get a little crowded.

So when we were planning a family trip one year, I called a friend of mine who works at a local business that adds all the bells and whistles to cars after they're purchased, and asked if I could rent one of their vans. At that time, they had a program where you could rent a fully loaded van in order to let you sample some of their work.

They don't do that anymore, and I think we're the reason.

First of all, I should say that I did have a premonition about this particular trip. I couldn't put my finger on it, but I just had a feeling that it was going to end up costing me more money than I had originally figured on. But since that usually happens on vacations, I didn't think much more about it. That is, until one fateful afternoon at the vacation condo pool.

So there we were, poolside, when Sherri suddenly decided that she wanted to go to the grocery store to get some supplies. Since I didn't want to go, I tossed her the keys. That's when the premonition returned. I thought to myself, *Little woman, big van . . . hmmm . . .*

Maybe this isn't such a good idea after all. But then I thought, *Hey, it's just the grocery store. What could happen? She can park the van way in the back and take up two or three parking spaces if she needs to.*

Yes, she could have done that.

When Sherri came home, she told me what she *had* done to the van.

"The guy who helped me get it off the wall that I ran into estimated it'll cost about two grand to repair it."

Get it off the wall—? I wanted to get upset; I really did. Two thousand dollars is a lot of money, and who knows, it could end up costing even more. The guy was only guessing. Still, instead of being angry, the only thing I could think about was how much leverage a mishap like that was going to give me! I could get away with almost anything from that point in the vacation on!

"It's okay, honey," I said. "These things happen. Vans like that cost only about fifty grand, you know, with all the bells and whistles on them. We're on vacation now. We'll worry about the repairs when we get home."

But when I walked out to look at the van and assess the damage myself, I was rendered speechless. Everything that my friend's employer had put on that side of the vehicle was gone. Sherri had not only damaged the van when she ran into the wall, but she had caused additional damage when she backed off of the wall. Without knowing the exact cost of these repairs, my leverage was limitless.

For the remainder of the trip, life was sweet:

"Where are the kids, Rick? . . . What do you mean, you don't know? You just let them run around without—?"

Sample Apologies for Men

- ❤ "Global warming? My bad. I'm sorry."
- ❤ "War in the Middle East? My fault. I'm sorry."
- ❤ "Traffic jam? I should have known it would be this way at nine o'clock in the evening. What was I thinking? I'm sorry."
- ❤ "Your friend has let you down? I'm to blame. I'm sorry."
- ❤ "Your mom is controlling? You're right. It's my fault. I'm sorry."
- ❤ "The dog tracked mud in on the carpet while I was at work? I should have known he was going to do that and stayed home. I'm sorry."
- ❤ "The kids got bad grades? Sorry. That would be from my side of the gene pool."
- ❤ "The housing bubble, the credit crunch, and the stock market crash? My fault, my fault, and my fault. Can you and the world ever forgive me?"

Sample Apologies for Women

- ❤ . . . "I'm sorry that you're not sorry."

"Hey, honey, how's the van doing?"

"I think I'll go grab me some ice cream, Sherri, if you'll stay here with the sleeping little ones."

"Hey, that's not fair. Why do I have to stay?"

"How's that van?"

"Okay, see ya."

It was beautiful, the kind of vacation a husband dreams about. I even got lost coming back.

"Well, this is just stupid, Rick. How could you—"

"Is it as stupid as wrecking the van?"

When we got home, I called my friend and asked, "Dude, how big are you in this company? Are you, like, a bigwig?"

"Yeah, I'm pretty high," he said. "Why?"

"Well, I hope you're real high."

He connected the dots—or I should say the *strewn auto parts.*

"You've wrecked the van?"

I confessed to my friend what had happened; then I added, "I know you have insurance and that's all covered, but you shouldn't have to turn this in. Tell me what I owe you."

He told me not to worry about it, which was more than kind of him. I thanked him for his kindness and forgiveness, and then enjoyed my leverage for a few more weeks at least.

Still, the next time we drive down to Pensacola and back, I think we'll be doing it in one of our own vehicles. They're already used to walls.

Living Like the Amish

I (Bubba) am still not sure why, but after years of marriage and getting me accustomed to how she does things around the house, one day Betty decided to turn the Bussey family world on its head and do everything differently. She decided that it was time to get domesticated. And by "domesticated," I'm not talking Martha Stewart. I'm talking Amish. Or Robinson Crusoe.

She signed up for Cooking Like Grandma classes. I wasn't used to this kind of eating. I was used to drive-thru lanes or food that could be prepared in a matter of minutes in the microwave. Like most of you, we live our lives on the run. We're usually rushing from this place to that place, grabbing a combo meal on the way.

But when Betty started cooking meals like Grandma, well, I've got to tell you, I loved it. Several of the local fast-food restaurants complained that Betty's decision to start cooking at home was singularly putting them out of business, but she ignored them and kept the gravy and biscuits coming.

The next domestic kick that Betty got on was sewing classes. Betty had never sewn before, but she wanted to learn how to do it. Her sales pitch for the expense of the class was that we could save money in the long run because she could then repair all our old clothing, rather than having the expense of buying new. Since I had a pair of

159

pants I'd been wanting hemmed anyway, I fell for the pitch—hook, line, and stitching.

What I soon discovered, though, was that the class was really just a cover for her to sew pillows and curtains. By my calculations, we already had enough pillows. And our curtains were fine, as far as I was concerned. But that's what the class turned out to be—a pillow-and-curtain class. I had written my check under false pretenses.

That's how they get you. Wives have a way of finding your Achilles' heel and then using it to trip you up. I wanted my pants hemmed, so I bit the bait.

Because I had been like Congress and not put rules on the bailout money, Betty got her class and we soon had piles of pillows, new curtains, and a lot of other nice things for around the house. *But my pants had no hem!*

I finally reminded Betty of the reason we got the sewing machine in the first place. "Betty," I said. "I thought the reason we got the sewing machine was so you could hem my pants and do a few more practical things for all of us."

Betty tried to divert my attention by showing off another new pillow that she had just sewn.

"That's great, hon," I said, wanting to be an encourager. "But when are you going to get to my pants?"

This went on for months, perhaps even years. Then one day Betty called me into the room and presented me with my hemmed pants. I usually wear shorts, but these pants—made of that kind of lightweight, parachute material—would now give me an option for more formal gatherings, where shorts might not be appropriate. I was so excited I couldn't wait to try them on.

Betty had done an outstanding job. They fit perfectly, and I couldn't even see the stitching. Betty was proud, but she said they weren't completely ready because she had to iron them now. (I didn't realize the Amish had electric irons, but Betty was willing to make that exception.)

So I handed the pants to her and changed back into my shorts.

While Betty was ironing, I was imagining how cool I was going to look in those pants. They were the hottest trend on the market; at least they were when I bought them. And now, I was mere minutes from finally getting to wear them. But when Betty came back into the room, she had the strangest look on her face.

She didn't say a word. She simply held up the pants to reveal a hole, as big as a softball, burned through them right below the knee.

"What happened?" I asked, blowing the smoke away from my face and stunned by the size of the hole.

"I started to iron them," she said, tearing up, "but I guess the iron was too hot for this kind of material, and it just melted a hole right through them!"

It was a Lucy and Desi moment. This could be why the Amish don't use electricity. Bad things can happen when items are plugged in. But then, Lucy's, I mean, Betty's creativity kicked in. So I now have a new pair of *shorts* that have a lot of time and money invested in them. They're my most expensive pair of shorts, and I love the lightweight, parachute-like material.

The way I see it, destiny was not working for me to ever have those pants. Maybe the fabric would have made my skin break out. Or the wind might have caught the parachute material and sent me flying up in the air, and I might have gotten hurt when I landed. Who knows? The fact is I just wasn't meant to have those pants.

And maybe we were both supposed to be Amish.

Dressing for the Occasion

I (Bubba) am going to try to handle the telling of the following story with the utmost delicacy. If, however, at any time you start to feel uncomfortable, please advance to the next chapter. But like I said, I will try to be sensitive.

As most married men know, there are certain items of clothing that a wife chooses to wear only for her husband. It's one of the perks of marriage. On one particular day, however, Betty gave me the surprise of my life. Allow me to set the stage.

Rick, Sherri, Betty, and I were attending an event where President George W. Bush was going to be speaking. We were all very excited that we were about to hear, and perhaps later meet, the president of the greatest country in the world.

When we arrived at the venue, we sat down and watched as several dignitaries were being seated in a roped-off area. Karl Rove, Ari Fleischer, even Sean Hannity were in the roped-off area. These people were on television night after night, and now here we were in the same room with them. We could hardly believe it.

But little did I know what else was going on "behind the scenes," so to speak.

Now, I am the first to admit that my wife, Betty, is hot. There is no other way to put it. She is a beautiful woman. At that time we had been married almost thirteen years, and on that particular night she had been in a quandary about what to wear to the event. You know how these things go.

After finally deciding on an outfit, Betty asked me if she should wear hose or not. I'll be honest with you—I am a leg man. In fact, it was Betty's legs that hooked me in the first place. Betty has very, very nice legs. And at this particular time of year, she had a bit of a tan going and was looking good. So I answered her question honestly and diplomatically.

"You know, Betty," I began, "whatever you want to do is fine with me. You have the legs that could go without hose if you'd like to. But I don't know of a bigger event than meeting the president. You might want to go with hose just because of the occasion; it is a more formal event. But either way is fine with me."

I knew from talking to Betty earlier that morning that she had already gone through one pair of panty hose while trying them on. They got hung on something and ripped. I'm not sure how that happens, but apparently nylons are very fragile. I don't know why women don't unite and look into the matter, because it clearly rings of a conspiracy.

Since Betty had already ruined her pair of nylons, I didn't know if she wanted to stop by the store to buy another pair or what. But I figured she'd let me know if she did.

For the record, I like the look of nylons. It's not a "has to be that way," but it is a preference. Apparently a lot of other people feel the same way, because nylons are still being sold in the stores. But I'm also fine with my wife going bare legged. Like I said, though, this was a more formal occasion.

At the event, I noticed Betty was wearing hose.

"I thought you tore your hose," I said.

"I wore the other pair," she said, matter-of-factly.

I got to thinking for a minute, *other* pair? But I thought she had said earlier that she didn't have any other panty hose. And we hadn't stopped by the store on the way to the event to buy a new pair. Then it hit me. Betty had to be wearing my Father's Day gift that she had gotten for me for later, if you know what I mean. *Betty had to be wearing the thigh highs!*

I looked at her with a questioning expression, and she just smiled back, innocently. From that moment on, my mind was not on the event. All I could think about was that my beloved wife was sitting next to me wearing thigh highs. My mind was as far away from world policies as it could get. I tried to act interested in what the president had to say, but my "Father's Day gift" kept getting in the way of world peace.

Even after the talk, as we were lining up to meet the president, all I could think about was my wife standing there next to me in thigh highs. That could also explain why I froze up when our turn finally came up. When the president reached out his hand to shake mine, I couldn't focus. My mind was mush. I couldn't put two words together.

Let me just say, for the rest of the evening, I sat real close to Betty.

I (Rick) had a similar situation with Sherri that night. The stock market was sinking, foreign affairs were a little shaky, but there was my wife, looking good, real good. All I could think about was, *Whoa, Sherri is going to really love me tonight for bringing her to this!* I was so distracted, I'm surprised I didn't say, "President Bush, it's great to meet you, but wow, my wife's looking fine today!"

When we got back to our homes later that night, the Busseys to theirs and the Burgesses to ours, you can bet we each had our own secret staff meeting.

The Rendezvous

In our church we have what we call "baby dedications." This is where we, as parents, dedicate our children back to God. It's our public acknowledgment of how God has entrusted us with our children to love and nurture, and how much we need the prayers of our church family as we spiritually mold our children for life and God's service.

On the Thursday evening before one of our baby dedications, I (Rick) and my wife, Sherri, attended a banquet that was held for all the parents. One of the staff pastors preached an outstanding message that you normally wouldn't expect to hear at a pre–baby dedication banquet, but it was a message that is crucial for all parents to remember. He spoke about how important it is to keep your spouse in his or her rightful place in your life, second only behind God.

Let's admit it, moms and dads; it's extremely hard to find time for your spouse when you've got a houseful of children running around. Let's also admit that none of us are prepared for how much we are going to love our children. The love of a parent for his or her child is overwhelming, so much so that if we're not careful, we can live a child-centered life, where the children become little gods to us and more important than both God and our spouse.

But the Bible is clear that it is God, our Creator, who is to have the number one position in our lives. After that, our number one earthly priority is to be our spouse. The children come in third. That doesn't mean we neglect them in any way or that we love them any less. It means that in order for us to be the parents we're supposed to be, we need to keep our priorities straight. Children can be adversely affected if the mommy-daddy, husband-wife relationship is at all compromised. They feel secure if there is a healthy balance there.

Don't feel bad. I've done it myself. I've lived the child-centered arrangement. I've allowed our children to become more important than my wife, and I'm sure she's done the same thing to me. But that's not how it's supposed to be.

So it was good that the minister reminded us about this and told us how we should be going on dates and spending time alone with our spouses. Since the birth of our newest baby, Sherri and I had been on only one date in nearly five months. So we agreed that we were going to go out together that Saturday night, the night before the baby dedication. It would just be me and her, and it was long overdue.

I took Sherri to her favorite restaurant. The weather was beautiful, and the food couldn't have been better. As we were sitting there, talking about life and how much we loved each other, Sherri came up with an idea—and what an idea it was! Dinner was coming to a close, but since it was only about seven o'clock, Sherri said one of those things rarely said in married life, but when you hear it, you can't believe your ears. My wife looked over at me and said, "You know, we ought to just go get us a room."

I almost choked on my last few sips of soda. But I wasn't about to pass up the offer. After all, I could see her reasoning—the babysitter was taking care of the kids, and they were probably having a great time. Since it was still early in the evening, none of them would be anywhere near going to bed, so why should we rush back home?

But to make sure I'd heard her correctly, I leaned in and said, "Serious business?"

"Sure," Sherri said. "Look, we're going to be back to parenting the minute we walk through our front door. But if this is the night it's supposed to be, it's too early to go back home."

Well, I did what any of you would have done in my shoes—I agreed with my wife. But there was one thing I forgot. I forgot that what Bubba and I do for a living is very public. There is, of course, both good and bad to this. It's fun when people recognize us out in public; it makes us feel good. We both love to sign autographs and talk about the show.

But not that night! That night we just wanted to be Mr. and Mrs. Average Tourist checking into a hotel.

That was not to be.

The first place we tried was sold out, so we drove on to another location because I wasn't about to let one little No Vacancy sign deter me. But when we got out of the car at the next hotel, the valet said, "Hey, you're from *Rick and Bubba*!"

"Uh . . . yes, uh, hi," I stuttered. "And this beautiful lady here is *my wife*" (emphasis on "my" and "wife").

Have you noticed how when you're totally innocent, but you worry that they're not going to believe you, you overexplain? I turned to Sherri and said, "Show him your driver's license, honey, so he can see you have the same last name as me."

But the valet didn't wait for Sherri. His curiosity was killing him. "But say, don't you live here?"

"Yes, I do," I said, trying to hurry the conversation along.

"But you're wanting the overnight parking?"

"No, that's not necessary," I said. "No need to take it too far away."

"Oh? Well, how long are you going to be with us?"

As the questions continued, I could sense Sherri starting to feel a little uneasy. I just wanted to get into the hotel before that valet ruined it for me.

"How long will you be here?" he repeated.

"Oh, about thirty minutes. Maybe an hour, if we cuddle."

Sherri didn't hear that part, so we were still good. She wasn't too embarrassed yet to call it all off.

We walked inside to the registration counter and, I kid you not, another man checking in at the desk said, "Hey, aren't you from *Rick and Bubba*?"

"Uh, uh, yes . . ."

"Well, how 'bout that? I'm here recording a gospel group. I live in Nashville. Say, when are you coming back up our way? Are y'all doing a broadcast here?"

"Not exactly," I said. I didn't see where I needed to give him more information. Luckily, the desk clerk came to my aid. Or so I thought.

"Y'all have any luggage? You want us to carry it up for you?"

"Luggage? Uh . . . naw, we don't have any luggage."

Meanwhile the valet is still holding up my keys and saying, "You sure you don't want me to park your car?"

"No, just hold it out there. In fact, just let it idle, if you would."

After the Alabama Inquisition was over, we finally got our room. But then, when we got ready to check out, I realized something else we had overlooked in our spontaneity—hair gel. When we left, our hair was sticking up all over our heads, exploding out in every direction. Needless to say, we walked out of that hotel as fast as we could. Out of the corner of my eye, I thought I saw a few people giving thumbs-up signs, and Sherri swears she heard a few giggles.

Luckily our car was still idling, and we could make a fast getaway.

All in all, it was a marriage date to remember, and let me tell you, at the baby dedication, I behaved very well. I was a happy, happy husband.

I don't know if it's true, but there's a rumor going around that the hotel even posted a sign that says, "Rick Burgess did *not* sleep here."

The Rematch

Sometimes you get more than just a date with your wife. Sometimes you get to be alone with her all weekend.

This was one of those weekends. I (Rick) had finally managed to arrange a romantic getaway at a beachside condo for Sherri and me. But as Sherri looked at the scenery and felt the soft sea breeze as it blew through her hair, she said, "Oh, Rick, the kids would've loved this!"

Not exactly the words I was longing to hear.

"We'll bring the kids with us the next time, Sherri. This is *our* weekend."

It wasn't her fault. There were kids all around the pool area where we happened to be at the moment, and it was hard for her not to have those maternal feelings. So I decided what I needed to do was get her away from there and go for a stroll along the beach.

"You know why we can walk on the beach?" I said, kicking sand up between my toes with each step.

"Why?" Sherri asked.

"Because we don't have our kids with us! We can do whatever we want to! You know what time we're going to have dinner tonight?"

"When?"

"Whenever we feel like it!"

But just as Sherri was beginning to catch on to our newfound freedom, something came over her. You see, Sherri tends to want to push every outdoor activity into some kind of exercise. So while I was contentedly strolling along the beach, Sherri decided that we weren't going fast enough.

"I don't guess you want to race me, do you?" she said.

"Race you? On the beach?" I couldn't believe what she was suggesting. Sherri was the 1987 Marshall County champion in the 200 and also in the 200 relay. With her as the anchor runner, her team won the whole county. She's very fast. And she was challenging *me* to a race?

It wasn't the first time. When we started dating, Sherri had challenged me to a race. At that time I weighed about 265 pounds, and I bragged that I could probably beat her in a sprint. I knew I didn't have a chance against her in a 200, but I was certain I could take her in a sprint. "You're crazy!" are the words I believe she used to accept my challenge.

Well, as it turned out, I wasn't crazy, because I beat her. The fact that she was wearing a dress doesn't give her any leverage. I still beat her. But she's been a poor loser ever since. That win has bothered her all these years. So it's understandable that she would want to try to redeem herself out there on the beach that day.

I tried telling her that I didn't like to run in the sand, but she was determined. She found a level strip of sand and then said, "Let's race down to that piece of driftwood over there."

While I was thinking about my answer, she took off. I tried catching up, mainly to protest. I didn't even consider that the race. But she did. And I lost.

Her shameless gloating over her win started to get to me. Even though you would think that someone as out of shape as I was, who had just run who knows how many meters in the sand, wouldn't want the word *sprint* to ever be brought up again. You'd think I would have seen how happy my lovely wife was over her win, fair or not, and just left well enough alone. You'd think I would have just let it go.

You'd think that, huh?

But inside, the Burgess competitive spirit started rising like Old Faithful. All I could hear was Bubba saying, "Hey, man, you just got owned by your wife."

I had to release some pressure on Old Faithful. So I said, "I don't guess you want to race again?"

"Oh, you want to race again?" Sherri said, almost in disbelief.

"Yeah."

Those of us who have been competitors, who have been warriors, understand this kind of thinking. We know that even though it looks hopeless, we can reach inside of us and grab pieces of our heart and will our way through to the finish line. Of course, there does come a point every so often when our hearts take a break and our legs just say, "Find me a sofa." But if we can make it past those critical points, we have a real shot at winning.

That day, aside from the heavy wheezing, I felt I really had a shot at winning the rematch. Besides, on the last race, Sherri had been the one to say "Ready, set, go!" That is a huge advantage. The person who says "Ready, set, go" knows when the "go!" is coming. That's unfair. So I told Sherri, "We'll run again, but this time, I'm going to say 'Ready, set, go!'"

She agreed, and at the "Go!" we took off, each of us running our fastest. I was stride for stride, and Sherri couldn't believe that I had come from being absolutely owned to within seconds being in the lead.

Then it happened. She took over my lead and passed me. But it was after the driftwood boundary, so I didn't figure it counted.

Claiming my legitimate victory, I announced, "Okay, that's it. I won that one!"

"*What?*"

"You added another ten feet. That's not fair. I had not prepared myself for that kind of distance. I ran only to the driftwood and then slowed down. You can't keep on running and then claim victory. I won fair and square."

She didn't want to argue with my obviously correct logic, so she compromised.

"All right," she said, "let's just race back the other way."

Even though I was the clear winner, I agreed. But that was when something happened inside of me, and there wasn't a thing I could do about it. What I did next nearly cost me the whole weekend, and looking back, I should have left well enough alone and just given her the driftwood win. I should have said, "Sherri, yes, you have beaten me in the sprint. Now, isn't this a great weekend? Congratulations to you, Sherri. Good job!" Then we could have continued with our romantic weekend.

But no, I couldn't let go of it.

The return match was on, and we took off running the other direction. Water was flying as we splashed along the beach, and in my mind, I thought I was running faster than I had ever run in my life. I was giving it everything I had. Old Faithful was putting on an impressive display.

At that point I don't know what happened. All I know is I saw Sherri lean in into my lane in order to get what I thought would be an unfair advantage. But you have to understand that I was a defensive lineman. There are certain spinal reflexes that kick in automatically because you've been trained to maul people on the football field.

My wife is all of five feet tall, but before I knew it, defensive line-man mentality kicked in. The last thing I recall seeing was the pink of her bathing suit as her body left the ground. When I snapped out of it, I realized I had put the forearm on my competition and sent her airborne.

But she was in my lane! Let's not lose sight of that fact. It was a clear violation, and I had every right to protect my lane. A lane violation gives me an automatic win, right?

Sherri disagreed. Spitting the sand out of her mouth and shaking it out of her hair, she rained on my parade. Right in the middle of my celebration, which involved jumping up and down and high-fiving total strangers on the beach, she protested the fairness of my move. I decided to take it up with some of the witnesses myself. I turned to them and said, "Have you ever seen a big man run that fast?"

One man answered, "Nope. I never have, especially when she was coming back down to earth. You got out of the way just in time, buddy."

See, they were all impressed with my speed.

Sherri came to her own defense. "Rick," she said. "I *(spitting more sand out of her mouth)* cannot believe that you *(spit, spit)* just knocked me down in what was supposed to be a friendly race on the beach!"

"You got in my lane, Sherri. That was a violation."

"Lanes? We're on the beach!"

"You still have a lane. It's imaginary, but you still have it."

"I cannot believe you just forearmed me."

"I'm sorry, but it was instinctive. So I won, right?"

"Rick, that was not a win."

"I crossed the line first, so it's a win."

I tried to get the crowd to cheer for me, but a couple of them were helping Sherri dress the scrapes that she had gotten in the fall. I saw she was winning the sympathy vote, so I didn't push it.

"You cheated, Rick," she said.

"Well, when you did the 'Ready, set, go' last time and got a jump on the race, I didn't cry about that." (Okay, I did whine about it to you here in this book, but at the time I let it slide.)

"Rick, they're not the same. I didn't clip your legs out from under you."

She was really going for details by then. So I dropped it. But for the record, all I did was protect my lane. I didn't mean for her to go flying into a somersault and land in the sand. That was unfortunate, and I do feel bad about that.

But I won!

Rick and Bubba's Ideal Date Nights

Not only do we recommend date nights and getaways with your spouse, but try to get away alone together at least two or three times a month if you can. And we do mean just the two of you, as husband and wife. It doesn't have to be an expensive date; it could just be a picnic. But make it special. Translation: *No Happy Meals*.

Nothing makes for a happier home than for a man and a woman who are madly in love with each other to be at the center of it. By continuing to date our spouses throughout our marriage, we keep the relationship alive and healthy. Your children want that. They long to know that their parents love each other.

Remember, too, that one day when your children are grown and on their own, it'll be just the two of you once again. You're going to have to actually converse with that person sitting across from you at the breakfast table. So don't let him or her become a stranger.

With this in mind, here are the leading contenders for Rick and Bubba's Ideal Date Nights:

1. Take your lovely bride to a big-time sports event that you wanted to attend anyway.

On its own, this is a great date. But to make this night even more special, here are some additional tips. My (Rick's) wife loves the "behind the scenes" sports stories. You know, Cinderella stories, like when one of the teams has never won a championship and this is their chance to make history. Or the quarterback's wife just got out of the hospital and he vows to win the game for her. Or the pitcher just came from the delivery room after the birth of his first son. He cut the umbilical cord and was then flown by helicopter to the game. Women love stuff like that. So do your homework. Research the game ahead of time and find out whatever backstory you can. If there isn't anything good to draw from, then recount the Babe Ruth story, being sure to tear up at the appropriate moment.

Caution: Do not consider a NASCAR event as a date. While it can certainly be a fun experience for you both, the romance is ruined by other men holding up signs asking for your wife's phone number.

2. Take your wife to a movie that you want to see.

This isn't as easy as it sounds because you will have to find an action film or a sports movie that also has some degree of a love story within the plot. It's the "spoonful of sugar" syndrome. The key is to get her to watch a guy movie by knowing the chick flick elements in the film. I (Rick) managed to pull this off successfully with the Dennis Quaid movie *The Rookie.* I focused on the husband-and-wife romance that was in the film and downplayed the sports element. I had to think outside the box to get past the title of the film, but I even managed to pull that one off, saying that "Rookie" was a pet name for the man, sort of like "sweetie" or "honey."

3. Go somewhere to eat out that is dark enough to be romantic but that serves great steaks.

These types of eating establishments can be tough to find, but they're well worth the effort. I (Rick) personally like Ruth's Chris Steak House and Shula's Steak House. Both of these restaurants provide a great atmosphere and at the same time give you enough to eat. There is just something about looking into your wife's beautiful eyes while chewing on a rib eye that makes you love her all the more. And who can top the romantic sensation that you get when you reach over to take hold of her hand, while gnawing on a T-bone? Does marriage get any more romantic than that?

4. Rent a hotel room for the two of you, even if you live across town.

I've already told you my story, but the idea deserves to be on this list. Drop the kids off at Nana and Grandpop's and then go check into a nice hotel and order room service, watch an old movie on the TV in the room, or just spend some quality time together doing whatever comes naturally. You can even make your own coffee in the room and, if there's a kitchenette, pop your own popcorn in the microwave. Let someone else clean up all the mess. Your goal is to spend some time together just hanging out and enjoying God's gift of marriage.

5. Take your wife to your local sporting goods store.

Not only will this give you a chance to check out the latest hunting gear, but you can show your wife how much you still care by holding the door open for her. And don't get impatient and shut the door before she has a chance to walk up to it, either. You don't know how far away she had to park.

6. Send the kids to Grandma and Grandpa's house, and then stay home and cook a romantic dinner for two.

This is one of my favorite date nights. It gives me a chance to prepare foods I like, and it guarantees that I won't miss any of my favorite TV shows because with the kids gone, I finally get control of the remote.

7. Take her to a concert.

Try to remember when one of your favorite groups that she can tolerate is performing, and then spring for tickets.

8. Have a mystery date.

Don't tell her where you're going. Just get in the car and start driving. That way you can impress her with your creativity, and you won't have to listen to her giving you directions on how to get wherever it is you're going.

9. Take her to a museum.

This is an especially good idea if you're starting to feel your age. Nothing will make you appear younger and more appealing to your wife than to be surrounded by mummies and old relics.

10. Stroll through the mall.

There is no better place for a husband to hold his wife's hand than at the mall. It keeps it from reaching for her MasterCard and VISA.

R – E – S – P – E – C – T

Aretha Franklin sang a song about it. Rodney Dangerfield never seemed to get enough of it. The Bible has plenty to say about it, too, especially when it comes to how husbands and wives treat each other. In Ephesians chapter 5, God uses the apostle Paul to instruct us on how marriage should be. Dr. Phil is good, but Paul's words don't have any commercial interruptions.

Respect and love go hand in hand. In fact, Paul, led by the Holy Spirit, wrote in the Scriptures that husbands are to love their wives as Christ loved the church. That doesn't sound like some halfhearted peck on the cheek when you leave for work in the morning, does it? It's not an *"I'm sorry I forgot our anniversary again"* card either.

Loving as Christ loved the church is a self-sacrificing, lay yourself down for, serve unreservedly, love unconditionally, forgive unrelentingly kind of love. Christ loved His church so much that He gave his life for it. Some of us can't even lay our sports page down for our wives. Or carry in the groceries. Or help with the dishes.

It's not easy to live up to Christ's example of "laying ourselves down." But Paul is saying that not only should we love our wives enough to be willing to give the ultimate sacrifice for her if called upon to do so, but that we should love her enough to want her needs met. That doesn't mean meeting her *wants*. Some husbands confuse the two and put their own *needs* aside to meet their wives' *wants*. Do that and you'll have an unbalanced relationship in no time. Paul said that husbands are to love their wives as they love themselves. He described it this way because most of us won't hate or mistreat our own flesh. So in order for us to love our wives with the kind of love that Paul is talking about, we need to love ourselves with that kind of love first. That's powerful, and often we forget it.

Problems will come into our lives and our marriage if we stop loving ourselves, or stop treating our own bodies with respect. Loving yourself isn't prideful; it's caretaking. If you don't take care of your own needs, how can you take care of your wife's?

But don't think that God doesn't have a standard for wives to live up to, too. The instruction that Paul gave to wives is for them to respect their husbands. Many women miss this part of his teaching because they are too busy highlighting the husband's instructions in their Bibles.

But respect is probably the number one need in a man. Even more than the other thing that you would think would be his number one need. Men want to be their wife's hero. Yet many wives find it easier to love, feed, or clothe their husbands than to show them respect. Why? Because when you simply love someone, you don't have to lay down your pride. When you feed him, you lay down only the fork and the grub. But showing someone respect means your own pride has to step aside, even when you don't want it to.

Paul nailed it. He knew our needs as husbands and wives. He was an equal-opportunity confronter. He was as straightforward with women as he was with men. Even though he was a single man, Paul understood the differences between the two sexes. He spoke to their inner cravings. Paul knew that men do not receive love the same way that women do. And he knew nothing strengthens a man more than being respected and revered by his wife.

I (Rick) can speak to the issue of respect personally. In the line of work that we do, many people either criticize us or pay us compliments on a daily basis. We get a lot of feedback. I also do many speaking engagements every year and have received both compliments and criticisms about my presentation. Like any human, I prefer the compliments. But I also know that criticism delivered in a positive and uplifting way can help me improve myself.

One thing I can tell you, though, is that all the compliments in the world cannot compare to receiving a single compliment from my number one earthly priority—my wife. When my wife tells me that I did a good job on something, it strengthens me like nothing else can.

Wife, you have the power to lift your husband up, but you also have the power to destroy him and render him useless in your home by your words and actions. It's not hard to make your husband the brunt of your jokes or complaints. We're easy targets. But you'll weaken him if you do, and you could also be weakening your marriage.

Something else I should say to all the men who are reading this is that we need to live worthy of that respect. (Wives, don't take this as your excuse not to respect your husbands. The position itself deserves your respect. And it's a commandment.) But husbands, use that knowledge to walk worthy of your wives' respect. And wives, live worthy of a love so great that your husbands would give themselves for it.

If husbands and wives could grasp these simple instructions, marriage would not be in the shape that it's in today. The divorce rate is as high in the church as it is outside the church—and growing. Something is broken, and it's up to us to fix it.

Husbands, love your wife as Christ loved the church, treat her as your own flesh, defend her and honor her. She will flourish and become the wife you've always dreamed of when she knows she's loved.

Wives, respect your husband and speak highly of him in front of others. He will slay dragons for you if he knows he is respected.

Most important, invite God into every aspect of your home and life. Read His Word together. The Bible has a lot of good advice on how to protect your marriage. Take advantage of it. It's the best marriage counseling service around, and it's free.

Shows Respect	Shows a Lack of Respect
Letting your husband order for himself.	Placing the order for the entire table, including your husband.
Letting your husband drive.	Having your husband sit in the backseat.
Bragging on how athletic your husband used to be.	Showing your husband's old football pictures and saying, "Guess who that is," then discussing how much weight he's gained over the years.
Allowing your husband to open the door for you.	Entering the establishment, going to the table, and already being seated and ordering before your husband even parks the car.
Being thankful to your husband for being a good provider.	Telling the kids, "We can't get that toy because Daddy doesn't make enough money."

Preparing your husband's plate for dinner.	Using the phrase "Get up and get it yourself."
Allowing your husband to read the Christmas story to the family.	Asking your husband to play the donkey.
Letting your husband tell a story in a group setting, without interrupting with USCs (Unnecessary Story Corrections).	Interrupting every other sentence with debatable descriptions that have no bearing on the story, but get you going on a rabbit trail and straight into an argument.
Allowing your husband to help the children with their homework, saying, "I'm sure Daddy knows the answer to that."	Uttering under your breath, "Like *he's* going to know the answers." (Confession: I, Rick, have been capped at second grade homework.)
Defending your husband in front of others.	Answering your friends' or family's accusations about your husband with the words "That's typical."
Allowing your husband to speak to the officer who just pulled him over.	Thanking the officer for pulling your husband over and then confessing for him the red light and stop sign he ran a week ago.
Listening intently to your husband as he retells the same funny story that you've heard multiple times.	Screaming out the punch line just to shorten the agony.

The Bible Study Visitor

It doesn't matter how long you've been married to your spouse, there could still be plenty about that person that you may not know. Take, for instance, my (Bubba's) wife, Betty. Betty is always surprising me with tidbits of additional information about her. For instance, I never knew how brave and determined she can be if called upon to take action.

I made my discovery the day Betty was having a women's Bible study at our house. Betty was right in the middle of a study on unconditional love when she looked up and noticed that our front door was cracked open just a little bit. Immediately my name popped into her head. *Bubba didn't shut the door all the way again,* she thought, and then continued the study.

Now, you've got to get this visual. There was Betty in the midst of about twelve women, all seated in a circle in the den. The Bible study came to a close, and they were milling around, still discussing the topic of the day.

Then one of the ladies looked over and saw a furry creature entering the room.

"Well, lookie there, Betty. Here comes your cat," she said.

Without turning to look, Betty replied, "Yeah, sometimes he comes in that way. That's fine."

But just then, someone else screamed, "That's not a cat! That's a chipmunk!"

Pandemonium broke out. Betty was still not putting two and two together. She thought that the cat had dragged in a chipmunk he had killed, you know, how cats do sometimes, like a trophy. Betty stood up to get a better look at the chipmunk and determine how big the plastic bag was going to have to be to discard of him. But this chipmunk didn't want to be discarded of. He was still very much alive!

So everyone started screaming, "It's alive! It's alive!" and began alternating between running from the creature and chasing it around the room. Before long, all these grown women had laid down their Bibles and were chasing that chipmunk around the dining room table, trying to corral it in one area so it couldn't get loose and run amok in the rest of the house. And one of Betty's six Christmas trees (that's not a typo—Betty really does decorate six of them) was in the foyer, right in the direct view of that chipmunk.

As Betty and the women were trying to swat the chipmunk with their hands, Betty suddenly remembered that she had once helped a woman at the ER clinic who had been attacked by a squirrel. It wasn't a pleasant memory, so Betty told the women that the best thing for them to do was to "take care of it," as in "eighty-six" it, as quickly as possible.

"But Betty," one of the ladies said. "We've just studied about unconditional love!"

Betty wasn't going to be deterred. She got the broom and said, "I don't think He meant for rodents!"

The chipmunk made a break for it and ran toward the Christmas tree. It took him several tries, jumping up and down, trying to land on one of the branches. He was a little smaller than most chipmunks, and I guess the trees from Hobby Lobby didn't provide as much friction as a tree from the forest, so he kept slipping off of it. It was like the scene from *Christmas Vacation*, only instead of the squirrel, it was his understudy, a chipmunk.

The little guy finally made it up the tree, and Betty went after it with a vengeance. You don't get between Betty and her Christmas trees! She started poking at it with the broom and, at one time, even tried talking it out. (I guess the unconditional love verses were getting to her.) When it looked like her plan was working, she told one of the girls, "Open the front door!" Then she jabbed him enough to get him to let go of the tree, and he fell back to the ground. They said he looked a little dizzy, but he got up and finally scampered out of the house.

I had been married to Betty a lot of years, and this was a whole different side of her that I had not seen before. I feel safer in our home now. I realize that if another critter happens to wander in, Betty can handle it. She's not one of these "jump up on the kitchen table and scream" kind of women. She's a creature of action. Unlike our cat. In fact, I think it was our cat who left the door ajar to begin with. He likes to torture the Bussey household. He probably brought it in and then stayed by the door to listen.

And, of course, laugh.

Enemies of the Mate

Marriages fail for many reasons. But it has been proven in situation after situation that *no reason* is above God's power to heal if both the husband and the wife are committed to saving the marriage, no matter what.

Unfortunately, at the first sign of trouble, a lot of outside voices start chipping away at whatever hope there could be for a reconciliation.

"I always knew he was a bum! Leave him!"

"You could have done so much better than her! Get out now, while the gettin's good!"

"Take my advice. I've been divorced three times. I know what I'm talking about."

Couples who decide to not listen to these negative outside influences and take their "for better or worse" to God, believing that He can heal their relationship—couples who admit that it takes two people to fail a marriage—will save themselves a lot of grief in the long run. Contrary to the "grass is always greener on the other side of the fence" and the "my happiness at any cost" mentality that is so prevalent today, divorce isn't the easy way out. A lot of destruction follows in its path.

But too often God's still, small voice is drowned out by the voices of others, well-intentioned or not—most often not. *"He doesn't treat you right"* will be the verdict given by someone who has *himself* been counseled on how he speaks to his wife. Someone who cheated on her own husband will warn, *"She cheated on you, and she'll never change."* Misery truly does love company. That's why it's best to not listen to Misery.

But if a divorce has already happened in your life, you can still learn from it. I (Rick) had a failed marriage. But I allowed myself time to heal before getting into another relationship. I was rebuilt from a broken man to the man God had always intended for me to be. Am I perfect today? Far from it. But from the first time I met Sherri, she saw what God saw in me. She saw my value when few others did, and she eventually helped me see it too. Even though I was a divorced man with two kids and was probably the farthest thing from her idea of Prince Charming, Sherri signed on for life with me. I'm so lucky and so very thankful that she did. Who knows where I would be today if it weren't for my wife?

❤❤

I (Bubba) can say that God has truly blessed me with a wonderful woman—my wife, Betty. We somehow ended up together after I stood her up for a date, and even after she gave me a wrong phone number. So many things came against us when we were dating, it's a wonder we *ever* got together. But we finally did, and we haven't looked back since. I knew beyond any doubt that Betty was the one for me, and she knew the same about me.

Marriage is what we make it. We men can make our wives feel wanted and loved, or we can make them feel insecure and lonely. Wives, you can make your husband feel honored and respected, or you can make him feel disrespected and useless. The power lies within each of us to make or break our marriage.

It bothers us when we see some wives tearing their husbands down in front of their girlfriends, mothers, or even their husbands' friends. Their actions turn a small problem into a bigger one and leave their mates feeling betrayed and disrespected. Then often what happens is a husband, in turn, subconsciously escalates whatever behavior the wife was complaining about. It's like a self-fulfilling prophecy. Talk like you have a terrible marriage, and you will have a terrible marriage.

By the same token, if a wife lifts up her husband to her girlfriends and family, then everyone will love and respect her husband, and he in turn will escalate whatever he's doing right.

The same holds true for the husband. If he lifts his wife up, both in front of her and behind her back, he might start seeing her behavior change.

If you truly need help with your relationship, then keep your complaints about your spouse before God and, if necessary, a marriage counselor. If you just want to gossip and don't care how quickly you destroy your marriage, then go ahead and bring in an audience.

The Bible says that life and death are in the power of the tongue. Are we speaking life into our marriages in our conversations with others, or are we speaking death?

A downside to all the instant-messaging, texting, e-mail, and cell phone capabilities available to us today is that we can share our thoughts as soon as they pop into our heads, before we've had time to think about them. In the past, people had to write and rewrite their letters, making sure every word was what they intended to say. Now we hit Send, and our words are out there, already starting their destruction.

We're going to ask you some hard questions right now. You don't have to answer them out loud, but if you value your marriage, you'll answer them in your heart.

Since you're the only one who is going to hear your answers, be honest. It doesn't help if you fool yourself.

- Could you give your spouse your e-mail password right now and be proud of every single word you've ever written about him or her?
- Could your spouse have listened in on your conversations at work, with your family, on the telephone, or at lunch with your friends and been proud of how you've portrayed him or her to others?
- Have the words you've spoken or typed torn down or built up your marriage?

Anyone who is married knows by now that they are not living with perfection. And if they're honest, they'll admit that they're not exhibiting perfection themselves. If you truly have problems in your marriage, it's best to talk to your pastor or a marriage counselor—not a girlfriend who has her own marital issues, or your mother, who never could stand your husband anyway. If people jump on the bandwagon when they hear your marriage is in trouble or immediately start matchmaking for your next relationship, chances are, these are not the people who are going to give you the best advice.

How many times has someone complained about her friend's husband—only to end up marrying the "cad" after they break up? There can be plenty of ulterior motives in a friend's, or even your family's, marital advice. Your mother may be complaining about your husband simply because she has lost her control over you. Or maybe her own marriage isn't in very good shape, so she needs to ruin yours to make her feel better.

The scenarios for ulterior motives are endless. The bottom line is this: If you want your marriage to be better, make it better. If need be, go to a marriage counselor, one that you both feel comfortable with, and share both sides of the story—your needs, your disappointments, and your failures. But also, share your good memories. Sometimes we get too focused on what's wrong with the marriage and forget all that's so right about it.

You've invested a lot in each other and your marriage. Don't let it go easily.

Top Ten Comebacks for People
Who Tell You to Give Up on Your Marriage

10. No, thanks. You'll have to destroy something else to make you feel better about your own life.

9. Let's face it, I married up. What are the odds of that happening again?

8. I'm not sure I can drive anywhere without her instructions.

7. Nooooo! I can't return to the Laundromat!

6. Do you think I really want to hunt and fish *all* the time?

5. But I get scared at night.

4. Then I really *will* have to lose weight.

3. It would be like *you* trying to give up gossip.

2. Say, I've got a better idea. Why don't you give up on hanging around me?

1. Take it up with God.

Things We Have Survived

As a couple, Sherri and I (Rick) have survived a lot of things. First, we survived taking the family to Disney World. Twice. We're proud of that. There's a certain kinship and bonding that takes place between a husband and a wife if they survive this sort of challenge. Believe us, the experience will be nothing like the couple you see on the commercials, the ones who laugh and skip hand in hand from ride to ride. For us, it was more like surviving being prisoners of war together. Don't misunderstand—it's not the amusement park's fault in any way. It is simply the dynamics of our family joined together with a mass of people, high Florida humidity, cotton candy, and ride lines the length of Hands Across America.

Sherri and I also survived the perm of 1994. This was almost a deal breaker. If you've ever come home and seen your wife crying on the sofa over a perm gone bad, you know what I'm talking about. And then, if you've risen to the occasion and provided her with the comfort she needs to forget all about looking like Gene Wilder in an electric storm and once again see herself as the beautiful woman she is, you can be proud.

We have survived countless birthday parties. I've got so many birthday party themes running in my head, I feel like Walt Disney. Princesses, pirates, Batman, Superman, Spidey, Scooby-Doo, Scooby-Don't—we've done them all. We even tried doing a carnival one year. You should have seen our backyard! Because I work in radio, the companies doubled the number of inflatables and kiddie rides that I had ordered. We had them all over the place!

The kids loved it and had a great time, but Sherri and I somehow transformed into carnival people during the event. I became the shirtless man trying to get kids seated and secured on the Tilt-A-Whirl. I still have night terrors over the event.

As fun as that party was, all the parents hated us for doing it. That's because it meant that they would have to try to top it for their own kid's birthday party. Apparently, we had set the standard too high. Even Bubba said, "Thanks, Rick. Now I'm going to have to book the Wiggles for our next birthday party!"

Sherri and I have also survived numerous meetings with teachers and principals, and the baking and bringing of countless cupcakes for class holiday parties. We've survived chaperoning field trips, trying to find a parking space or a seat at school programs, and all those fund-raising candy bar sales (we usually win for having bought and eaten the most).

We've survived Little League too. Trust us, a marriage will be tested when a husband turns into a crazy, screaming dad on the Little League field. Hundreds of games later, I admit I tend to get a little too excited over the kids' sports games and may, at times, even go too far. (I *have* to admit it—Sherri's got the videotapes.)

We have survived Christmas morning, when the kids have opened, from grandparents or aunts and uncles, gifts bearing those horrible words "Some assembly required." (A parent would never buy a toy with such profanity emblazoned across the box.)

We've also survived moving. For the record, I *hate* moving. Most statistics show that finances and intimacy are the two leading reasons for marital conflict. But I say it's moving. The arguments and bickering that can erupt during a move, whether across town or the entire country, are historic. And it all begins with the packing process.

"Why don't we give this away?" is asked way too often by your wife, and always while holding up *your* stuff. Sherri and I can never seem to agree on what stays and what goes, and so we end up needing to rent a second moving truck just to move all our stuff. We have been known to have such big disagreements during a move that they have forced us to enact what we call the "attic rule." The attic rule goes something like this: "If the item in question didn't come out of the attic the entire time we've lived in the house we are now moving from, it is not to have the luxury of being moved to the new home." Makes sense, right?

We've survived vacations. How many times have you returned from a vacation only to need another vacation to recover from the one you just took? I believe this is due to setting unrealistic expectations. You see the family on the brochure, and you believe that is your family. It is not. I know it hurts, but the sooner you accept this, the easier it will be on you.

No matter how hard you try to reenact the scene from the brochure, your kids will not look or act like those kids. Your wife will not be smiling like the woman on the brochure. And you will not look like the dad. The dad in the brochure doesn't have the *"Sorry, but do you have another credit card we can use?"* look on his face. He isn't cleaning up the spilled soda in the backseat of the car. And his wife isn't holding a map, pointing to the highway that he should have taken, instead of the one that he is on. There is no cow loitering on the road in front of the car in the brochure, either.

Yes, we've survived vacations, and we have even survived the mandatory family vacation picture on the beach. You may have survived one of those yourself. What is it about women that, as soon as they step foot onto a sandy beach, makes them decide that a family portrait must be taken? I submit to you that the collapse of the vacation begins at that precise moment. For the rest of your time together at your beach house or your hotel, or whatever, you will be running from store to store, trying to find the perfect white outfits for everyone to wear for the photo.

Then at the appointed day and time, everyone will be gathered together on the beach and forced to look natural—and happy. When kids who have just been whisked away from building sand castles or body surfing are told to "not get dirty" and to smile a mother-approved smile, there is no way the moment isn't set up for disaster. And when the pictures are developed, there is also no way that dad isn't going to be blamed for whoever isn't looking at the camera or who got into a fight with his or her sibling and is frowning, or who has dirt on his shirt.

As the father of five kids, I can't begin to tell you how many doctor visits we've survived, too. Most memorable are the ones with the obstetrician. Like I've said, I don't understand why a husband has to be so involved in these visits. He is never treated like he's really welcome. In fact, he's often given a look of "How could you?" by everyone in the waiting room. His only saving grace is the fact that all the other husbands in the room are being given the same look.

If you're a new father, I warn you that no book, no friend, and no television show on pregnancy can ever prepare you for that awkward moment when the doctor first walks into the examination room and rolls his stool around to a location that you feel more than a little

Whatever the "worse" is in your marriage, you can be a supportive partner for your spouse. All you have to do is determine to be attuned to the other person's needs.

During this time of loss, I have watched my wife cling to her God, the great I Am, and be comforted by the Holy Spirit. She has set aside her own pain to be about the business of spreading the gospel of Jesus Christ and allowing Bronner's death to count for something. We both live and cling to chapter 8 of Romans—all of it, not just a few verses. We also cover each other with John 16:33: "I have told you these things, so that in me you may have peace. In this world you will have trouble. But take heart! I have overcome the world" (NIV). We quote these verses to each other often.

Sherri has had her down moments too. I will never forget the day when I walked into the kitchen and could see that my wife was feeling overwhelmed. The grief of the loss of her baby was hitting her so hard that she could barely stand. She asked me to tell her again why this had happened and what God was doing to use this tragedy to change people's lives around the world.

In typical maleness, I said, "Honey, I have already told you all this." She looked at me with a tearstained face and said, "Well, then tell me again!" Sherri needed to be reminded how God was bringing good out of such pain. She knew that He had promised that, but she needed her husband to remind her of it. And God clearly was bringing good out of bad, more than we could have ever imagined. At that moment, though, all Sherri was seeing and feeling was the pain.

Don't get me wrong. Sherri knows her Bible. She spends a lot of time studying God's Word. Still, no matter how well she knew the truth, discouragement was attacking her. She needed a covering from her husband. She needed me to bathe her in the Scriptures again and again, until the pain could subside and she could focus once more on the bigger picture.

Too many times we husbands complain about our wives' shortcomings when we should be sharing the Word of God with them and living it out daily in front of them. And too many times wives take their troubles to their girlfriends first, instead of to their mates and to God.

Sherri and I try to do better at that now. We try to sense each other's vulnerabilities and be a shield for that person whom God has given us to love. We also try to live one day at a time. We have no choice. It's all we can handle right now: just putting one foot in front of the other, one day, one step, one breath at a time.

But we had no forewarning.

None of us knows what the future is going to bring. So we all need to live each day as it comes, appreciate its blessings and survive its challenges. We need to not sweat the little things. Our focus is heaven now. We know we have a beautiful treasure named Bronner Burgess waiting for us there, and that inspires us, as a husband and wife, to honor our Savior through this loss.

Bronner's life has already had an impact on a lost and dying world. The thousands of calls and letters we have received from friends, fans, and total strangers telling us how Bronner's story has affected them have been overwhelming.

One day not long after Bronner's death, Sherri called to tell me that she had a dream of seeing Bronner in heaven. He was swimming in the River of Life, smiling and looking happy and content. That dream gave her hope, but she said it also showed her something that is even sadder than the earthly death of our son.

"What could possibly be sadder than losing Bronner?" I asked.

"We will get our Bronner back when we get to heaven. But when God's children reject Him and perish, He never gets them back. That is the saddest thing, and it happens by the thousands every day."

Sherri's right. As hard as it's been to say good-bye to Bronner on this side of eternity, there are so many more who have yet to hear the gospel. So now Sherri and I work side by side, doing everything we can to present the good news of Jesus Christ to as many people as we can. That is what keeps us going as a couple and as a family. Our goal is to have an impact for the kingdom of God, and not waste our time fretting over things that just don't matter.

Our marriage isn't merely surviving after the death of our sweet child; it's thriving. Every day I am blessed to live the truth of the Bible, where God says that a man who has a godly wife has a good thing. I have a good thing. And I am so very, very thankful for her.

After Fifty Years of Marriage . . .

We look forward to the day we can both celebrate fifty years of our marriages. At that time, I (Rick) want to be able to look back and say that I was the type of husband that the Bible called me to be. I want to be proud of the way I've treated my wife. I want her to be able to say that she was my number one priority in life. I want her to know beyond any doubt that she was adored, respected, and loved, and had a husband who defended her and placed her on a pedestal. I want to have successfully loved her as Christ loved the church.

I want to be able to say I was a hands-on father to my children, not a dad that the kids barely knew. I want to have been involved in every aspect of my kids' lives.

I want to have led my household in the example that Christ gave us men to lead—by serving. I want my wife and my children to have felt like I washed their feet daily, in humility and service. I don't want any of them to feel that I demanded their respect, but that I earned it, so they gave it to me enthusiastically. I want it to be said that I was a benevolent leader, that I in no way exasperated my family.

I want to reach my fiftieth anniversary loving my wife more on that day than I did on the day we married.

I (Bubba) hope the same thing for Betty. I hope that she will be glad she gave me another chance and married me. I hope that she will look back on fifty years of marriage, recall all the good times and bad times, the ups and the downs, the times we didn't know where the next meal was coming from, and the times of plenty, and all those Bible studies in the book of Solomon, and say, "I'd do it all over again."

Marriage isn't perfect. If that's what you're striving for, you're going to be disappointed. Marriage is overlooking all those annoying things your spouse does that get on your nerves, it's forgiving him for when he's let you down, and forgiving her for the same, and it's helping you both to become the best person, as well as the best husband or wife, you can be. It's surviving the tough times and enjoying the good times with every fiber of your being.

Thank you, Sherri and Betty, for hanging in there and giving us an almost nearly perfect life together.

BONUS

Rick and Bubba's
The Book of Blame

Introduction

On our radio show, we have often referred to *The Book of Blame*. What exactly is *The Book of Blame*? It is one of the most closely guarded secrets in society today. Think Kentucky Fried Chicken protects the identity of their eleven herbs and spices? That's nothing compared to the effort that has gone into keeping the contents of *The Book of Blame* secret.

Until now, only women were aware that *The Book of Blame* even existed. We still wouldn't know about it had I (Rick) not found it one day while looking through Sherri's hope chest. (If you're not familiar with what a hope chest is, then let me try to explain. A hope chest is a trunk that many girls receive as a gift to start saving up things for their marriage to Prince Charming—things like dishes, satin sheets, and apparently, a leather-bound copy of *The Book of Blame*.) It seems the book has been handed down from mother to daughter over the centuries, being updated periodically by someone who refuses to be named. Until I found it nestled in that hope chest, no man had ever seen it, although we had long speculated about its existence.

Within its covers lie the secrets and rules for the wife's blaming everything that may go wrong in life on the husband. Contrary to what you may have thought, a young bride cannot just start blaming things willy-nilly on her partner. There is a proper way to do it, learned from years of trial and error.

So why hasn't the existence of this book been written about in fairy tales? Where was the paragraph stating that Cinderella would one day blame Prince Charming for everything that had gone wrong in her life—as would Snow White, Sleeping Beauty, and every other princess who has come down the pike? The writers seem to have skipped over that little detail. They left it at ". . . and they lived happily ever after," with no mention of *The Book of Blame* anywhere. That seems a bit deceptive to us.

When I first discovered the book, I immediately showed it to Bubba; he was already aware of its existence. Although he had never personally seen a copy, he was sure that Betty had one in her possession because she seemed to quote from it from time to time. He couldn't be sure, but since the words that Betty used seemed strangely similar to the words he had also heard Sherri say on occasion, and his mother, and mine, as well, he was suspicious that they were all reading from the same source.

Now that we have finally unearthed a copy of this mysterious book, we are both determined to do our civic duty and bring *The Book of Blame* out of the shadows and into the light. We are bringing it to the attention of the entire world, but most especially it's provided here as a resource for all you husbands who have lived in the dark for far too long.

With the publication of these secrets, we are saving a multitude of men from continuing to naively walk into situations unaware of the dangerous landmines that await them. But without their own personal copy of *The Book of Blame*, how could they possibly know what they are up against? Without full access to this book and the secrets that lie within its pages, they are doomed to live under the false assumption that someday they will be in the right and blameless.

How sad is that?

Marriage isn't easy. Sometimes the waters get a little turbulent. A husband needs to know ahead of time what he is going to get blamed for so that he can be prepared with an appropriate apology.

We realize, though, that now it will be just a matter of time before all of our wives come out with a new version of *The Book of Blame*. Once they know we are onto them, they will have no choice but to change all the rules. But for now, this revelation should help husbands everywhere—for a while anyway.

So without further delay, here it is, direct from the official Rick and Bubba offices in Alabama, the long-awaited, never-before-published, official, unedited, complete, and indisputable *The Book of Blame*!

But first—please sign the following confidentiality agreement.

The Book of Blame
Confidentiality Agreement

(Before proceeding, please read and sign the following.)

I, _____ , do solemnly swear to keep the contents of this book secret. I understand the serious ramifications that could result from the leaking of such sensitive information and will guard these ageless secrets with my very life.

_____

(Signature)

The Book of Blame

Article I

Whereas it is the consensus among women not only that men possess the gift of mind-reading, but that they operate under 100 percent accuracy down to the very last detail, a husband shall know beyond a shadow of a doubt what a woman wants for Christmas, and he will also know her current size, the color that she would like it to be in, and whether or not she needs a pair of shoes to match.

Article II

It is hereby declared that no matter how many people live in the home, no matter how many computers are running, how many stereos and television sets are left on, or how many electric guitars are blaring, the high utility bill will be blamed on Dad for having plugged in the $4.98 rechargeable screwdriver he got in his stocking last Christmas.

Article III

Let it be known that any unsuccessful search for a vacant spot in any parking lot on the face of the earth is the husband's fault and is just cause to bring up the perfect spot he drove right by during the Black Friday shopping spree of 1982.

Article IV

In the event of a parent-teacher meeting where heredity issues are brought up, defer all remarks to the husband's side of the gene pool only. Why bring up more than one side at a time? It'll only confuse things.

Article V

Should you be pulled over for an unsafe lane change and speeding, explain to the officer that it was because your husband was telling you to pass the car in front of you. Leave out the part about how that was last week and you were stuck behind a tractor.

Article VI

The reason you are overdrawn in the bank will always be the pair of socks your husband bought, but didn't tell you about. *"The house payment would have cleared if it weren't for those socks!"* In situations like this, it is best not to bring up your hair appointment or the luncheon with your girlfriends. Stay focused.

Article VII

Any meal at any restaurant that is not to your liking is your husband's fault. If he selected the restaurant, it's his fault. If he let you select the restaurant, it's his fault for allowing you to pick a substandard one.

Article VIII

If you are late to any event, it is your husband's fault. If he had not gone on out to the car and started the engine to wait for you there, you would not have taken so long getting ready. (If you say this quickly in the heat of the moment, it almost makes sense.)

Article IX

Let it be further known that if there isn't any hot water left for your shower, it is your husband's fault. The dishwasher that you started ten minutes ago—and the washing machine that is also going—have nothing to do with the situation. It is your husband's fault. Hold him accountable.

Article X

If your 401(k) tanked in the recent financial crisis, it is your husband's fault. Even though it surprised most of Congress, he should have seen it coming.

Article XI

When a husband and wife are lost, the man shall always be blamed for the incident. Never mind that the woman is directing him from a map or that the woman herself is behind the wheel; the husband will always be blamed. It has been this way since the invention of the wheel. Don't fight it.

Article XII

If there is such a thing as global warming, it is your husband's fault.

Article XIII

If any food item is overcooked, undercooked, or burned to a crisp, it is your husband's fault, even if he is nowhere near the vicinity of the kitchen. He may not even be home at the time. He may be at work or away on a business trip. But it will still be his fault. We're not sure how he accomplishes this, but until our investigation is complete and we have all our evidence in place on this, trust us—it is his fault.

Article XIV

If you cannot find the keys to your car, your jacket, your glasses, or your Bible, it is your husband's fault. Even if they turn up where you in fact put them last, he probably moved them temporarily while you searched for them and then put them back. Why husbands do this sort of thing is still being researched, but they do it, we know they do it, and thus, it is their fault.

Article XV

If you happen to trip over a toy that the children left on the living room floor, it is your husband's fault. Had he not bought them the toy two Christmases ago, the child would not have the toy to begin with, and thus the toy never could have ended up on the floor.

Article XVI

Any dissatisfaction that you may have with your own family and any baggage from your childhood is your husband's fault. This is something with which your family will readily concur, and with that many people in agreement, it has to be so.

Article XVII

The 2008 world financial crisis was your husband's fault. How many times did you tell him to use your own bank's ATMs? The extra $36 in charges threw off your budget, which caused you to spend less at the grocery store, which threw off their budget and caused them to either declare bankruptcy or change themselves to a bank and request a bailout from the government. They chose the latter, which increased the deficit by more than $2 trillion, which we, as well as our children and grandchildren, will ultimately have to repay. All because your husband wouldn't listen to you! See? It's all his fault.

Article XVIII

The fluctuating price of gas is your husband's fault. If he wouldn't waste so much of the precious commodity running the engine while in the car in subzero temperatures, waiting for you to finish your shoe shopping, there wouldn't be a gas shortage or price hikes.

Article XIX

If your hairstylist uses a new product that causes your hair to fall out and leaves you looking like you vacationed at Chernobyl, it is your husband's fault. Had he not volunteered to watch the kids, you never would have kept your appointment.

Article XX

If you cannot fit into your favorite pair of jeans, it is your husband's fault. He has been secretly shrinking the jeans by rewashing them in hot water when you're not home. He is a sick man.

Article XXI

If you come down with any cold, flu, sinus infection, hives, fever, or any number of other physical ailments, it is your husband's fault. Never mind that he himself is not sick—he is the carrier.

Article XXII

If you gain weight, it is your husband's fault. Had he eaten his half of the cakes, pies, cookies, and brownies that have passed through your kitchen over the previous few months, you never would have gained that weight.

Article XXIII

If you have never used your gym membership that you bought four years ago or have yet to take a single step on the StairMaster you bought last summer, it is your husband's fault. If he had only discouraged you from exercising, instead of encouraging you, you would have had your incentive to work out.

Article XXIV

If you run out of hangers on your side of the closet, it is your husband's fault. He has secretly been stealing yours. How those four new outfits that you just bought for yourself found hangers is not important. Your husband is taking your hangers when you're not looking. Probably on the same night that he's shrinking your jeans.

Article XXV

If you happen to hit the side of a wall with a rented van, it is your husband's fault. Had he not rented the van in the first place, you could have hit the wall with your own vehicle and saved all the paperwork.

Article XXVI

If you run out of shampoo, it is your husband's fault, even if he has his own bottle of shampoo. He has secretly been using yours.

Article XXVII

If you forget to mail the house payment, it is your husband's fault. Had he not forgotten to buy stamps the last time he was at the post office, you would have seen the book of stamps on the table by the door, which would have reminded you that something needed to be mailed. You would have then checked the bill drawer and discovered the house payment was not there, which would have caused you to look in the console of the car, and you would have discovered the unstamped, unmailed mortgage payment.

Article XXVIII

Any meteor or comet that is hurtling toward earth is your husband's fault. If it hits your house, it is especially his fault because that was the house that *he* picked out. You wanted the other model on the next street over, remember?

Article XXIX

If you run out of gas in your car, it is your husband's fault. Had he not reminded you to stop and fill it up the last time you used it, you would have known that it was up to you to remember and not have depended on future reminders from him.

Article XXX

If you can't find a hotel with a vacancy, it is your husband's fault. Had he ignored your protests and gone ahead and pulled into that teepee motel he passed four hours ago, you'd be asleep by now.

Article XXXI

If a check that you've been expecting gets lost in the mail, it is your husband's fault. We're not sure why. It just is.

Article XXXII

If the Internet is down, it is your husband's fault. It doesn't matter whether the Internet is down in your entire region, in most of your state, or in the whole world; it is your husband's fault. What he did to crash the Internet, only God knows. And maybe Al Gore.

Article XXXIII

If you can't find a parking space at the mall, it is your husband's fault. After all, didn't he already pass three perfectly good ones? Sure, they were at a different mall, but what's that got to do with anything? If in doubt about this, refer to Article III. The mall is definitely *somewhere* "on the face of the earth," so it's his fault.

Article XXXIV

If you are in a traffic jam, it is your husband's fault. He never should have listened to you and taken that route in the first place.

Article XXXV

If your grocery store shopping cart doesn't work properly, it is your husband's fault. He accepted the first one you pulled out and should have known better.

Article XXXVI

If you lose the reception on your cell phone, it's your husband's fault. He should have anticipated that problem and pulled over to the side of the road. Or stopped and built a new cell phone tower.

Article XXXVII

If your dishwasher overflows, it's your husband's fault. He never empties it, and it has to do something to get noticed.

Article XXXVIII

If you hit a pothole in the road, it's your husband's fault. He should have warned you about it . . . on the cell phone . . . from his office.

Article XXXIX

If your flight is delayed, it's your husband's fault because he drove too slowly getting to the airport—no, wait! That would be if you *missed the flight*. Oh, well, it's his fault anyway.

Article XL

Be it known herewith that all hurricanes Category 3 and above are your husband's fault. His overwatering of the lawn caused extreme changes in the atmosphere. (How many times have you warned him about that?) He wouldn't listen, and now look what happened.

Article XLI

If there is an all-city blackout, it is your husband's fault. He was no doubt trying to point out the potential risk of leaving too many lights on around the house. He's so dramatic.

Article XLII

If NASA can't launch a rocket at its scheduled flight time, it's your husband's fault. His cell phone was probably causing interference.

Article XLIII

If your coffee's too hot, it is your husband's fault. After all your years together, he should have known that if the coffee was too hot, he should have gone to your default beverage and ordered a soda. If the soda machine wasn't working, he should have known to default to milk, unless they didn't have 2 percent, and then it's water. It's no wonder some days you feel like you're living with a stranger!

Article XLIV

Sonic booms are always your husband's fault—at least until one of his "pull my finger" tricks has been completely and undeniably ruled out.

Article XLV

If you can't get to sleep at night, it's your husband's fault. Never mind that he has already moved downstairs and is now sleeping on the sofa. After all these years, the sound of his snoring has been trapped inside the walls of your bedroom and now resonates from them like the sound of ocean waves does in a seashell.

Article XLVI

If your area is in a drought and has to ration water, it is your husband's fault. Had he not taken so long to get around to fixing the leaky faucet in your bathroom, the planet would have more H_2O.

Article XLVII

Childhood issues with your mother, your teachers, or bullies in your grade school are all your husband's fault. Just because he wasn't in your life at that time doesn't mean he's not to blame. Don't be naive.

Article XLVIII

All weather issues related to El Niño are your husband's fault. El Niño is a guy.

Article XLIX

Every wrong decision you've ever made, either on your own or as a couple, is your husband's fault. It's just easier that way.

Article L

The fact that Rick and Bubba even got their hands on a copy of this centuries-old, closely guarded, secret book is your husband's—no, actually, *that* one would be *your* fault. You didn't hide it well enough. Don't blame *everything* on the poor guy!

Acknowledgments

We want to thank:

First and foremost, *Jesus Christ*, the greatest hero of all time and the Savior of the world.

We would also like to thank:

Martha Bolton. Thanks for taking our random, unorganized thoughts and putting them on paper.

Thomas Nelson Publishing. Thanks for believing in us and turning two C students into *New York Times* best-selling authors. (Our English teachers never saw *that* coming!)

Bob Carey and everyone at Syndicated Solutions. Keep moving the chains and expanding the Rick and Bubba radio world.

Ray Nelson and everyone at Cox Broadcasting. Thanks for being the type of company and individuals who believe there really is such a thing as a win-win scenario.

David Sanford, Elizabeth Honeycutt, and the rest of the team at Sanford Communications, Inc., a special thanks. And congratulations on "merging" with the great folks at Credo Communications LLC. We look forward to working together for a long time to come!

Everyone who makes it happen at Rick & Bubba Inc.: Calvin "Speedy" Wilburn, the real Greg Burgess, Ryan Greenwood, Scott "The Tech

Guy" Ferguson, Super Tom Scott, Mark Gentle, Don Yessick, Ken "Bones" Hearn, and all interns past, present, and future.

Don Juan DeMarco. We miss you! Thanks for all your years of service.

All of our families who support us through thick and thin, and who have to go back to sleep after we wake them up early every morning when we go out the door to do the morning show.

All of you who pray for us, support us, love us, and hold us accountable.

Everyone around the world who listens to the *Rick and Bubba Show.* God has used *you* to change the world.